LEONARD J. AF
MORMON HISTORY 1
No. 12

Brigham Young, the Quorum of the Twelve, and the Latter-day Saint Investigation of the Mountain Meadows Massacre

by

Thomas G. Alexander

September 21, 2006

Sponsored by

Special Collections & Archives
Merrill Library
Utah State University
Logan, Utah

Copyright © 2007 Thomas G. Alexander

ISBN 978-0-87421-687-5
Distributed by
Utah State University Press
Logan, Utah 84322-7800

Introduction

F. Ross Peterson

The establishment of a lecture series honoring a library's special collections and a donor to that collection is unique. Utah State University's Merrill-Cazier Library houses the personal and historical collection of Leonard J. Arrington, a renowned scholar of the American West. As part of Arrington's gift to the university, he requested that the university's historical collection become the focus for an annual lecture on an aspect of Mormon history. Utah State agreed to the request and in 1995 inaugurated the annual Leonard J. Arrington Mormon History Lecture.

Utah State University's Special Collections and Archives is ideally suited as the host for the lecture series. The state's land grant university began collecting records very early, and in the 1960s became a major depository for Utah and Mormon records. Leonard and his wife Grace joined the USU faculty and family in 1946, and the Arringtons and their colleagues worked to collect original diaries, journals, letters, and photographs.

Although trained as an economist at the University of North Carolina, Arrington became a Mormon historian of international repute. Working with numerous colleagues, the Twin Falls, Idaho, native produced the classic *Great Basin Kingdom: An Economic History of the Latter-day Saints* in 1958. Utilizing available collections at USU, Arrington embarked on a prolific publishing and editing career. He and his close ally, Dr. S. George Ellsworth, helped organize the Western History Association, and they created the *Western Historical Quarterly* as the scholarly voice of the WHA. While serving with Ellsworth as editor of the new journal, Arrington also helped both the Mormon History Association and the independent journal *Dialogue* get established.

One of Arrington's great talents was to encourage and inspire other scholars or writers. While he worked on biographies or institutional histories, he employed many young scholars as researchers. He fostered many careers as well as arranged for the publication of numerous books and articles.

In 1973, Arrington accepted the appointment as the official historian of the Church of Jesus Christ of Latter-day Saints as well as the Lemuel Redd Chair of Western History at Brigham Young University. More and more Arrington focused on Mormon, rather than economic, historical topics. His own career flourished by the publication of *The Mormon Experience*, co-authored with Davis Bitton, and *American Moses: A Biography of Brigham Young*. He and his staff produced many research papers and position papers for the LDS Church as well. Nevertheless, tension developed over the historical process, and Arrington chose to move full time to BYU with his entire staff. The Joseph Fielding Smith Institute of History was established, and Leonard continued to mentor new scholars as well as publish biographies. He also produced a very significant two-volume study, *The History of Idaho*.

After Grace Arrington passed away, Leonard married Harriet Horne of Salt Lake City. They made the decision to deposit the vast Arrington collection of research documents, letters, files, books, and journals at Utah State University. The Leonard J. Arrington Historical Archives is part of the university's Special Collections. The Arrington Lecture Committee works with Special Collections to sponsor the annual lecture.

Thomas G. Alexander is the Lemuel Hardison Redd Jr. Professor of Western American History, Emeritus, at Brigham Young University, where he also formerly directed the Charles Redd Center for Western Studies. He is the author, coauthor, or editor of some twenty books, including *Mormonism in Transition: A History of the Latter-day Saints, 1890–1930*; *Things in Heaven and Earth: The Life and Times of Wilford Woodruff, a Mormon Prophet*; and *Utah, The Right Place: The Official Centennial History*.

Dr. Alexander appreciates the assistance of Richard E. Turley, Jr., Ronald W. Walker, and Glen M. Leonard. Brian Reeves helped him by supplying copies of documents. Others who assisted include Mel Bashore, Chad Orton, Chad Foulger, Michael Landon, Steve Sorensen, Brent Reber, Barbara Brown, and Alison Gainer. Thanks also to Ron Read of the LDS Church Historical Library and Dixie

Dillon of the Huntington Library for supplying photographs for the presentation and LaJean P. Carruth and her staff for the transcription of short hand notes and entries and Deseret Alphabet entries in various diaries and documents.

Brigham Young, the Quorum of the Twelve, and the Latter-day Saint Investigation of the Mountain Meadows Massacre

*A*s early as May 29, 1857, Utahns had begun to believe their lives stood in peril. Word seeped in that President James Buchanan had dispatched an army of two to three thousand troops "to the Territory."[1] Throughout the summer, Brigham Young, as incumbent governor of Utah Territory and president of the Church of Jesus Christ of Latter-day Saints, met in council to discuss the pending military invasion with various civic and church leaders, including members of the Quorum of the Twelve, his counselors, Territorial Delegate John M. Bernhisel, and Salt Lake businessman Feramorz Little.[2] On July 12, after meeting with Little, Young wrote that he wished "to avoid hostilities with the United States," but would "draw my sword in the name of Isreal [*sic*] God" before he would "See this people Suffer as they have done heretofore."[3]

In a dramatic confirmation of previous intelligence, Abraham O. Smoot, Judson Stoddard, Porter Rockwell, William Garr, and Elias Smith rode into the Twenty-fourth of July celebration in Big Cottonwood Canyon. They told those assembled that the administration had cancelled Utah's mail contract and ordered twenty-five hundred troops to Utah. The couriers reported that throughout the United States a "feeling of Mobocracy is rife," and "the constant cry is kill the Mormons." Defiantly, Young responded "Let them try it."[4]

Confirmation of the impending invasion did not change the plans the territorial leadership had begun to formulate. During the spring and summer of 1857, the community leaders met in council. We should understand that the LDS church functioned as what John Gunnison called a "theo-democracy," not as a dictatorship of Brigham Young or anyone else.[5] As such, the central leadership or general authorities left considerable leeway for local initiative in most matters while conducting periodic investigations to assist in solving problems, gathering information, and offering counsel and, when they believed conditions required, releasing, disfellowshipping, or excommunicating offenders.[6] Since the church was a theo-democracy, local Saints could oppose unpopular policies, and in certain critical conditions, they forced the leadership to change or abandon such programs and policies.[7]

Meetings on the pending invasion included members of the Twelve, Young and his counselors, and people with information. Together they made plans to contend with the army. Their plans included recalling missionaries and settlers from outlying regions, calling for assistance from outside Utah, seeking allies, alerting the church membership to prepare for the invasion, and evacuating Utah settlements, if necessary.[8]

As the leaders mobilized the community for war, Young and others criticized some local gentiles (as Mormons and non-Mormons called non-Mormons in the nineteenth century) while attempting to maintain good relations with others of them. For example, Young leveled a blistering attack on Charles Mogo, a deputy U.S. Surveyor who came under serious criticism from the Latter-day Saint community for his work. After Mogo wrote a letter explaining his point of view, Young responded with a letter of apology. Later investigations by federal officials showed that the surveyors had conducted shoddy surveys which had to be redone.[9]

Young also achieved some success in reining in Mormon hoodlums who started using the martial preparations as a license to prey on non-Mormons. On August 19, he "took measures" to stop "Some men" who were causing trouble with non-Mormon business people. Commenting on his policies, Young said he intended "to give my enemies fair warning." He wrote, "I wish to meet all men at the judgment Bar of God without any to fear me or accuse me of a wrong action." The diary entry is a bit unclear, but the latter comment may have referred to a possible fight with the army.[10]

Prudently, in view of the relative poverty and weakness of the Mormon community compared with the rest of the United States, he sought allies. He exchanged correspondence with Pennsylvania aristocrat Thomas L. Kane, a prominent political figure sympathetic to the Mormons but associated with President James Buchanan, a fellow Pennsylvanian. Though he made friends with some non-Mormon merchants like William Bell, he realized that he could expect little tangible support from them or from most Euro-Americans outside the Latter-day Saint fold.

In planning for Utah's defense, Young and other leaders understood the antagonism that existed between American Indians on the one hand and overland emigrants and the army on the other. Young deplored the indiscriminate killing of Indians. In spite of building settlements on Ute, Shoshone, Goshute, and Paiute lands and frequently fighting battles with these peoples, the Latter-day Saints continued to view the Indians as children of Israel and fellow citizens of God's kingdom.[11]

Given Mormon belief in American Indians' descent from the House of Israel, it is not surprising that church leaders and members sought and expected to cement an alliance with them. The information that the Mormons received led them to believe that they could hold the army at bay but that doing so would lead to an extended siege of their intermountain kingdom. To prepare to feed the community during the anticipated siege, Young broke with his previous policy of discouraging Indians from raiding emigrant trains. He sent Dimick Huntington and other emissaries to encourage Indians to steal cattle on the northern and southern overland routes. He expected to store stolen livestock and local grain in the mountains to feed the Euro-Americans and the Indians during the starving time that they expected to accompany the siege. On September 1, he and other leaders met with a group of Pahvant Ute and Paiute leaders to encourage this policy.[12]

Recognizing that Young had previously counseled Indians to promote good relations with emigrants, some Indians commented that his advice constituted a reversal of former policy. Young justified the change on the ground that Utahns, whites and Indians alike, needed to store food for the prospective siege.[13]

Armies have frequently lived off the bounty of their enemies. Alexander the Great fueled his march to Babylon and India from local populations, and William T. Sherman used a similar tactic in his campaign from Atlanta to Savannah in November and December 1864. A dearth of food and water has often forced besieged people to capitulate to the enemy. To avert this possibility, church leaders intended to feed the besieged people in part with cattle taken from overland emigrants.

In order to secure the cattle, Young meant to rely on Numic allies. These included the Utes, Shoshones, Gosiutes, and Paiutes. With the exception of some Pahvant Utes, however, most of the other groups, including other Utes, generally declined to ally themselves with the Mormons. On the other hand, the cattle-theft policy succeeded partly with some Southern

Paiutes who lived in close proximity to southern Utah communities, such as Cedar City, Harmony, Washington, and Santa Clara.[14]

We should understand that some Numic people had engaged in livestock theft during periods of intense overland migration. For many American Indians, such activity seemed small recompense for the use of their lands and resources. Such theft had become most intense outside areas of Mormon influence, particularly on the northern overland trail from City of Rocks to the Humboldt Sink.[15]

Prior to September 1857, the Mormons had relied on secondhand information about the plans of the United States Army. On Tuesday, September 8, however, Capt. Stewart Van Vliet came to Salt Lake City to purchase supplies for the army. Offering to furnish nothing but lumber to the troops, Young liked the young officer, but he reemphasized his disdain for and fear of the Buchanan administration and the army.[16]

Then, in a startling turn of events, as the leaders met in council on Thursday, September 10, James Haslam entered the meeting, bringing a letter from the Cedar City stake president, Isaac C. Haight. Haight asked whether they should chastise the Baker-Fancher Party. Figuratively hitting the ceiling, Young responded with orders to allow the party to pass, forbidding Haight to interfere with subsequent parties and castigating him for effectively declaring martial law. Young told Haslam that the party had a "perfect right to pass."[17] Perhaps referring to his Indian policy, however, he wrote that the "Indians we expect to do as they please."[18]

Some commentators have argued that Young already knew about the plans for the massacre and that, indeed, he had ordered it. Federal Judge John Cradlebaugh and Bvt. Major James H. Carleton believed that they had found evidence of Young's culpability in statements from Paiute chiefs Jackson and Tonche who said that an Indian interpreter from Salt Lake named Huntington had brought a letter from Young telling them that they should help massacre the emigrants. Jackson also told Carleton that Lee and Haight had led the massacre.[19] The letter, if it ever existed, has disappeared, no corroborating evidence has appeared for Carleton and Cradlebaugh's statements, and it is doubtful that their Paiute informants could then read English. Moreover, Haight did not arrive at the meadows until Saturday morning, after the massacre had taken place. In addition, Jackson also said that although John D. Lee "was there," as they were, like them, he refused to participate in the massacre, "being, like themselves, afraid."[20] Jackson also blamed Lee for the death of his brother at Mountain

Meadows. In 1866, Judge John Titus reportedly collected "false affidavits," connecting Young to the massacre.[21]

Significantly, contrary to authors who have insisted that the interview with Van Vliet changed Young's policy, the young officer's visit actually reinforced Young's previous plans.[22] On Sunday September 13, he gave a stinging tabernacle address in Van Vliet's presence. Afterward, Young and other leaders met with Van Vliet, again emphasizing their fear of the army. Young told him that the Utahns "would . . . have received their governors & [civil] officers if they had sent them here without an Army." He said he believed that the army would hold the Mormons captive "while others run their red hot Iron into us & then kill us." Because of this prospect, he said, "we will not have neither their soldiers Armies no[r] officers any more here at all."[23]

Reinforcing these plans, after four days of discussions with Van Vliet, Young wrote letters to church leaders in the eastern United States, Canada, and Europe emphasizing the alliance with the Indians— "cousin Lemuel," he called them—and urging lay members and missionaries to gather to Utah with their weapons. When they arrived, Young wrote, the Saints must build up a defense against the army and prepare to abandon settlements and retreat to siege quarters if necessary.[24]

Then on September 14, the day that Van Vliet left, Young met again in council with Heber C. Kimball, Daniel H. Wells, members of the twelve, "& several others." The council adopted a proclamation of martial law that they dated September 15. The cover letter sent to local leaders with the proclamation reiterated the need to prepare to abandon settlements and to give emigrant trains passes and let them travel in peace.[25]

Within a week, however, he began to hear that a terrible tragedy, contrary to his instructions, had taken place in southern Utah. On September 20, Ute chief Arapeen, brother to the late chief Wakara, stopped to see Young. He told the Mormon leader "that the Piedes had killd the whole of a Emigrant company & took all of their stock & it was right."[26] On September 28, Leo Hawkins, a clerk in the Church Historian's Office, recorded that "reports reached town that the companies of Cala[fornia] Emigrants" consisting of "100 men & 1000" cattle "were all used up by the Indians" at Mountain Meadows.[27]

On September 29, John D. Lee arrived in Salt Lake City where he met with Young and Apostle Wilford Woodruff. The story he told partly confirmed Arapeen's account and Hawkins's report. In Lee's case, however, he told

Young that he had come to the site after the massacre and helped bury the emigrants.[28] Young came to work at 7 a.m. that morning, but Lee's story of blood and gore apparently so sickened him that at 11 a.m. he had himself driven to his upper mill at the mouth of Parley's Canyon, "his health being feeble."[29]

In 1870, Lee insisted that he had told Young the truth except for "one thing." He insisted that in reporting to Young he had assumed responsibility for the massacre himself. In 1876 and afterward, either Lee or his attorney, W. W. Bishop, wrote that Lee "believed" that the orders for the massacre had come from Young through George A. Smith.[30]

Historians face serious difficulties in assessing the validity of these conflicting accounts. Both Wilford Woodruff and John D. Lee had motives for misrepresenting what Lee told Woodruff and Young. The Council of the Twelve and the First Presidency excommunicated Lee on October 8, 1870, and particularly after his conviction for murder in 1876, he had a potent motive to justify his actions by blaming Young, who had abandoned him, and assigning blame partly to others. Woodruff, of course, had the motive of protecting the general church leadership from blame.

Using accepted historical documentary analysis, Lee's alleged confession must lie under a cloud. Woodruff wrote the earliest account of Lee's report. In 1870, thirteen years after the meeting Woodruff attended, in a discussion with Young that followed his excommunication, Lee told Young that he had told him everything except one thing in 1857. Lee's own journal account of Young's reply at that meeting says that Young told Lee that he had not learned "the particuelars [sic] until recently," which meant that he had not learned them at the 1857 visit.[31] Moreover, Lee's confessions, issued as *Mormonism Unveiled,* were edited and published posthumously by his lawyer W. W. Bishop, so we do not know that the words are actually Lee's. Also, in *Mormonism Unveiled,* Lee or Bishop claimed that Brigham Young told him not to tell anyone about the massacre, yet he gave his account in the presence of Woodruff, who wrote his holograph diary entry shortly after Lee reported to Young. In addition to his holograph journal, written in September 1857, Woodruff in 1882 testified in an affidavit that Lee had laid the entire blame on the Indians and taken credit for leading the party that buried the murdered emigrants.[32] Following the massacre, according to Lee or Bishop, the participants "voted unanimously that any man who should divulge the secret, or tell who was present, or do anything that would lead to a discovery of the truth, should suffer death." Lee's journal contains numerous entries in which he denied any culpability.[33] In a

June 1895 discussion with Abraham H. Cannon, massacre participant Samuel Knight said that from hearing conversations between the leaders he concluded after the massacre that "none of the general authorities of the Church had sanctioned or encouraged" the massacre and that they "knew nothing about the massacre until . . . after the terrible event had occurred."[34] This analysis has led me to believe that in 1857 Lee lied to Young and Woodruff and that he assigned blame to the Paiutes, as Arapeen and the earlier "reports" had done.

Significantly, shortly after Lee left Salt Lake City, Young received a letter dated September 30 from George W. Armstrong, Indian agent at the Spanish Fork Indian Farm, also assigning blame to the Indians.[35] We do not know conclusively the source of Armstrong's information. He may have heard of the events from Lee.[36] On the other hand, as Indian agent at Spanish Fork, Armstrong may have got the information from Indians who, as Arapeen and Jacob Hamblin reported, had already begun to circulate reports of the massacre. Significantly, in December 1857 and January 1858, on the basis of the reports he had then received, Young repeated the story of an Indian massacre, as told by Arapeen, Lee, and Armstrong, in letters to church members in southern California, to Commissioner of Indian Affairs James Denver, and to others.[37]

Shortly after Lee's report, however, word reached Salt Lake City that non-Mormons in California blamed the massacre on "the Mormons." Already dubious about the Saints remaining in southern California as war fever raged, Young now released them from their mission and urged them to return to Utah for their own safety.[38]

A number of federal officials supported the California gentiles' assertions of Mormon culpability, though unlike Cradlebaugh and Carleton, a number did not tar Young with the blame. On December 4, the same day that Young wrote to the southern California Saints reporting the story of an Indian massacre, Garland Hurt, an Indian agent who had fled from the Spanish Fork Farm, blamed the Mormons and Indians. He wrote on the basis of reports from Utes that the Paiutes and Mormons had carried out the massacre, the Paiutes at the urging of the Mormons through John D. Lee.[39]

Hurt's incomplete, but partly correct version received further elucidation from Utah Superintendent of Indian Affairs Jacob Forney. Young most likely dismissed the report by anti-Mormon Hurt and, particularly, those authored by Cradlebaugh and Carleton, who erroneously blamed him. Forney, who was often friendly with the Latter-day Saints, wrote reports in

May and August 1859. Significantly, Forney, like Hurt, laid the blame on a small group of Southern Utah militiamen and the Paiutes rather than on Brigham Young.[40]

In June 1858, Young received evidence from Jacob Hamblin contradicting the story of an Indian massacre that Arapeen, Lee, and Armstrong had told him. On June 20, Hamblin visited George A. Smith at the Church Historian's Office and told him of the massacre.[41] The two went to see Brigham Young, and Hamblin gave him an account.

We do not know everything Hamblin told Young, but on November 13, 1871, he sent a letter to Brigham Young, and he filed an affidavit on November 28, 1871, both of which probably paralleled his earlier report.[42] Hamblin said that he had met Lee near Fillmore on September 24 as the latter came north to report to Young. He said Lee told him that he and "the Indians had commenced" the attack. Lee reported that the "immigrants were all wiped out excepting a few children." When Hamblin asked why, Lee said, "They were enemies to us, and that this was the beginning of great and important events." Apparently fearing Cedar City and other southern Utah settlements stood in danger, Lee argued that the massacre had become necessary to protect "the lives of the Brethren." In his testimony at Lee's second trial, Hamblin also said that Lee had told him that he had killed a woman. He also testified that although he later learned that other white men participated, Lee told him at this time that he and the Indians were there alone.[43]

Hamblin also said he received a justification similar to Lee's from William H. Dame, the Iron County militia commander and Parowan stake president, and after he arrived at his ranch, he learned from his wife, Rachel, that the young children had been rescued and the emigrant party's goods plundered.[44] Rachel asked him if the massacre "was right, and counciled by Church authorities, I told her *No*, that it was one of the worst Massacres on the annals of history."[45] Dame defended the massacre as necessary to clean up "a bad job" begun by "Lee and the Indians," and protect the local brethren from Buchanan's wrath. Hamblin emphatically rejected such a justification as unworthy of a God-fearing people.[46]

We know of other possible sources for Hamblin's report. He said his initial information came from "a rumor of it among the Indians." He also might have learned more from his wife, Rachel; his adopted son, Albert, who said that he watched the massacre; or from his brother, Oscar, who was present during part of the assault.[47]

We do not know all that Lee told Hamblin, but we know that Hamblin said he learned more in a visit to Virgin City (Pocketville) while gathering the surviving children in 1859, a year after his report to Young and Smith. He told Deputy U.S. Marshal William Rogers that what he learned had surprised him. He said that he would report the information to Governor Cumming, but he did not.[48] If Lee had told Hamblin everything in 1858, what he learned at Virgin in 1859 most certainly would not have surprised him.

Whatever else Young told Hamblin, he also told him to keep this matter quiet until they could get a "court of justice" to investigate the massacre.[49] Hamblin did so, and in fact, his subsequent reports often treated the violence at Mountain Meadows as an Indian massacre.

Young may have learned more about the massacre later in June. On the twenty-fourth, he met with Dame and Nephi Johnson in Provo, to hear a report on their exploration of the west desert and a potential settlement 147 miles west of Parowan. The written report does not mention the massacre, but Dame may have discussed it. Nevertheless, it seems probable that Johnson did not talk about the matter because Young learned his version much later.[50]

In writing about the massacre and Young's role in it, authors have taken diverse positions. Writing in the nineteenth century, Orson F. Whitney placed the principal blame on John D. Lee, Philip Klingensmith, a few militiamen, and the Indians.[51] In his reply to Whitney, Robert N. Baskin, quoting his closing argument in John D. Lee's first trial, arraigned "Brigham Young as an accessory of the massacre, because considering the power he had over his people, no man, bishop, or any other subordinate officer, would have dared to take such an important step, or engage in such heinous scheme, if he hadn't the direct or implied sanction of the head of the church." Moreover, he alleged that Brigham Young had conducted no investigation.[52] In the mid-twentieth century, Juanita Brooks argued that Young and George A. Smith did not order the massacre, but that they "did preach sermons and set up social conditions which made it possible," and that Young "was an accessory after the fact, in that he knew what happened, and how and why it happened."[53] A recent book on the massacre by Sally Denton insisted "within the context of the era and the history of Brigham Young's complete authoritarian control over his domain and his followers, it is inconceivable that a crime of this magnitude could have occurred without direct orders from him." Will Bagley argued that "The emigrants fell victim to Brigham Young's decision to stage a violent incident that would demonstrate his power to control the Indians of the Great Basin and stop travel on the most important overland roads."[54]

None of these authors have presented any direct evidence, evidence beyond a reasonable doubt, or even a preponderance of circumstantial evidence that Brigham Young ordered the massacre. Authors like Denton, clearly unfamiliar with nineteenth-century LDS and Utah history, do not understand the limits of Young's power or the examples of local initiatives, especially in war time. Moreover, his actions after the massacre provide evidence that he did not understand at first why or how it had happened. In faulting Young for not investigating immediately, Baskin and some other authors ignore that during the fall of 1857 and the winter and spring of 1858, Young believed it necessary to protect the people of Utah from an army that he considered "a mob" sent to murder Mormons. Under the circumstances, until he received Jacob Hamblin's report in June 1858, he accepted without a direct investigation the early reports assigning blame to the Indians.

Most importantly, the following narrative will show that beginning in the summer of 1858, after the efforts of a number of people—including Thomas L. Kane, peace commissioners Lazarus Powell and Ben McCulloch, and Governor Alfred Cumming—had tethered the army, Young and other church leaders began what became an extended investigation of the massacre.

Because of contradictory reports about the causes of and responsibility for the massacre, the church leaders conducted at least three and perhaps as many as five investigations. These led during Young's lifetime to the release of at least five of the participants from their church positions, to the excommunication of two of the leaders, and to the reinstatement of one of them. Most significantly, Young and other prominent church and civic leaders offered both physical and monetary assistance to capture and try those accused of perpetrating the massacre. Their efforts to assist the responsible federal officials in the investigation failed, not because the church leaders stonewalled, but because Utah's U.S. marshal and chief justice torpedoed them by refusing to accept the offered assistance.

After receiving Hamblin's 1858 report, Young and others had heard conflicting stories that he apparently hoped to resolve by sending apostles George A. Smith and Amasa M. Lyman to investigate the massacre as part of a tour of the southern settlements. Leaving Salt Lake City on Thursday,

July 15, 1858, Smith and Lyman preached and questioned as they traveled. Sermonizing and investigating took them through the settlements around Mountain Meadows: Cedar City, Pinto, Hamblin's Ranch, Santa Clara, Heberville, Washington, Toquerville, Harmony, and Hamilton's Fort. Smith and Lyman remained in Harmony until the afternoon of August 6, when they traveled on to Cedar City.[55]

From Cedar City, Smith sent a letter to the Church Historian's Office on August 6 indicating that he and Lyman learned little about the real story of the massacre before they reached Parowan on August 8. With the exception of Henry Lunt, massacre participants shepherded them through the region. They reached the massacre site on July 29 and, like others, the sight of scattered bones and decomposing corpses sobered them.[56] After arriving in Harmony, Smith, Lyman, and Haight met with Lee. The apostles arrived in Cedar City at about 3:30 p.m. on August 6 and left for Parowan on August 7.[57]

The dating is crucial because Lee's journal reports a hearing in Cedar City that began on August 5 and continued on August 6 until "near Night," and that it included in addition to Smith and Lyman, apostles Erastus Snow and Charles C. Rich, who had come to southern Utah to collect Deseret currency.[58] By contrast, Henry Lunt dated an investigation by apostles Lyman, Rich, and Snow "in relation to many complaints made against Isaac C. Height . . . and Philip" Klingensmith on August 23 and 24, long after Smith had left for Salt Lake City.[59]

The dates and days in Lee's reports of the investigation were mismatched and written with a number of different pens. Significantly, parts of the entries were inserted in small letters, as though they were crowded in. Moreover, Lee's journal contains no entries from August 9 through September 14, 1858, except a summary entry that deals with construction and harvesting and mentions September 10.[60] < > Since many of the entries elaborate on items mentioned by Lunt, Lee seems to have written them at a later date, misdated them, and squeezed part of them in. Most significantly, if the four apostles had already cleared these matters on August 5 and 6, the three apostles would have had no reason to return for a second hearing.

After Smith and *Deseret News* reporter James McKnight arrived in Cedar City at 3:30 p.m. on August 6, they prepared an account of the massacre.[61] They probably wrote for the Church Historian's Office and perhaps the *Deseret News*, rather than Young, since clerical notations suggest that he never saw it. Most significantly, the document contains a later notation by Smith which says "This statement is doubtless incorrect as to the dates, as the massacre must have occurred earlier in the month, say about fifteen days."[62] Smith probably made this notation because of information he and Lyman learned during an investigation in Parowan, August 8 through 12.

The August 6 document calls the murders an Indian massacre.[63] The report begins by noting that "rumor reached Cedar by Indians" on Tuesday "that an emigrant train had been attacked in camp by the Indians on Monday." Lee continued to maintain till the end of his life that he was not at the Meadows during the attack on Monday.[64] The account then follows the Haight and Lee's concocted report as recorded by Wilford Woodruff. It claims Indians died from "the poisoning of springs." Cedar City raised men "to go and," try unsuccessfully to "conciliate the Indians." Unable to help the emigrants without endangering their own lives, "they returned to Cedar."[65]

"On Friday evening," according to the report, "Wm. H. Dame, Isaac C. Haight and a party of men" went to the Meadows to try "to put a stop to the fight . . . ." They arrived about daylight, Saturday, too late to save the emigrants from "The Indians."[66] This report shows that the apostles' investigation to that point led them to believe Lee rather than Hamblin.[67]

On Saturday, August 7, Smith and Lyman left Cedar City for Parowan.[68] On Sunday, August 8, they attended an evening council meeting in which local leaders leveled numerous complaints against Dame.[69] On Monday, August 9, at 2:00 p.m., Smith and Lyman opened hearings on the charges.[70] One charge accused Dame of supporting "the man who [brutally] assaulted" William Leaney. Sent by Dame, Barney Carter, Dame's brother-in-law, had battered Leaney for aiding William Aden, a member of the Baker-Fancher train. This charge probably raised questions about the massacre.[71]

The investigation which ended on August 12, included Smith, Lyman, and church leaders from Parowan. Significantly, however, the two apostles also summoned Isaac Haight, John M. Higbee, Nephi Johnson, and Samuel D. White from the south.[72] All of them, except possibly White, had participated in the Mountain Meadows affair. The minutes omit the massacre, and Smith and Lyman exonerated Dame in a hearing that Haight characterized as "Patient but Painful."[73]

Nevertheless, the hearing which left Smith "sick from confinement of Council Room," probably uncovered evidence that Lee and others had been at the Meadows during the massacre. Lyman returned to Cedar City on August 15 to sermonize. Smith, who had family in Parowan, remained until August 17 when he left for Beaver.[74] Before leaving, however, Smith wrote a report to Brigham Young on the massacre, apparently based on findings revealed by the Dame investigation.[75] In his report, Smith excerpted portions of the article he and McKnight had written on August 6, but the tone and substance had markedly changed. Smith had learned that the massacre took place the week of September 6 through 11, rather than September 21 through 25. The August 6 text described the massacre as "The Emigrant and Indian War." The August 17 report called it "the horrible massacre at the Mountain Meadows."[76] On August 6, when Smith believed the Haight-Lee version, he thought the Indians had sought revenge for "the death of several" of their tribe.[77]

By contrast, the August 17 report explained that the emigrants had outraged the Cedar City settlers, leading them to join the Indians.[78] At Fillmore, the emigrants, Smith wrote, had "threatened the destruction of the town, and boasted of their participation in the murders and other outrages that were inflicted upon the Mormons in Missouri and Illinois." They poisoned springs and a dead ox at Corn Creek. Poison from the ox killed Proctor Robison and injured John Ray's wife,[79] He did not attempt to reconcile the dates of these poisonings with the passage of the emigrant party.

"While passing through the lower settlements," he wrote, "the emigrants . . . threatened to stop" further down the trail, and "fatten their stock," to supply the troops. Afterward, they intended to "help to kill every 'God damned Mormon'. . . ." Supporting their claim, the emigrants said "that some four or five hundred dragoons were expected through on the Fremont trail, [which passed through the plateaus to Parowan] whom they would join."[80]

While the August 6 account merely mentioned Dame's arrival at the Meadows after the massacre, the August 17 letter argued for his innocence. Apparently Dame had managed to clear himself by pointing to his efforts at the same time to save the Turner-Dukes party from a Pahvant attack at Beaver.

Haight seems to have deflected blame from himself by placing Lee and some other unnamed persons at the scene during the massacre rather than afterward, as Lee had told Young and Woodruff.[81] The August 17 report said "that John D. Lee and a few other white men were" at the Meadows, "during a portion of the combat . . . ." Conceding his information was still incomplete, he said that he had not found out why they were there, "or how they conducted, or whether indeed they were there at all" for what he still thought erroneously was ultimately a Paiute massacre.[82]

John D. Lee Journal, August 5 through September 14, 1858

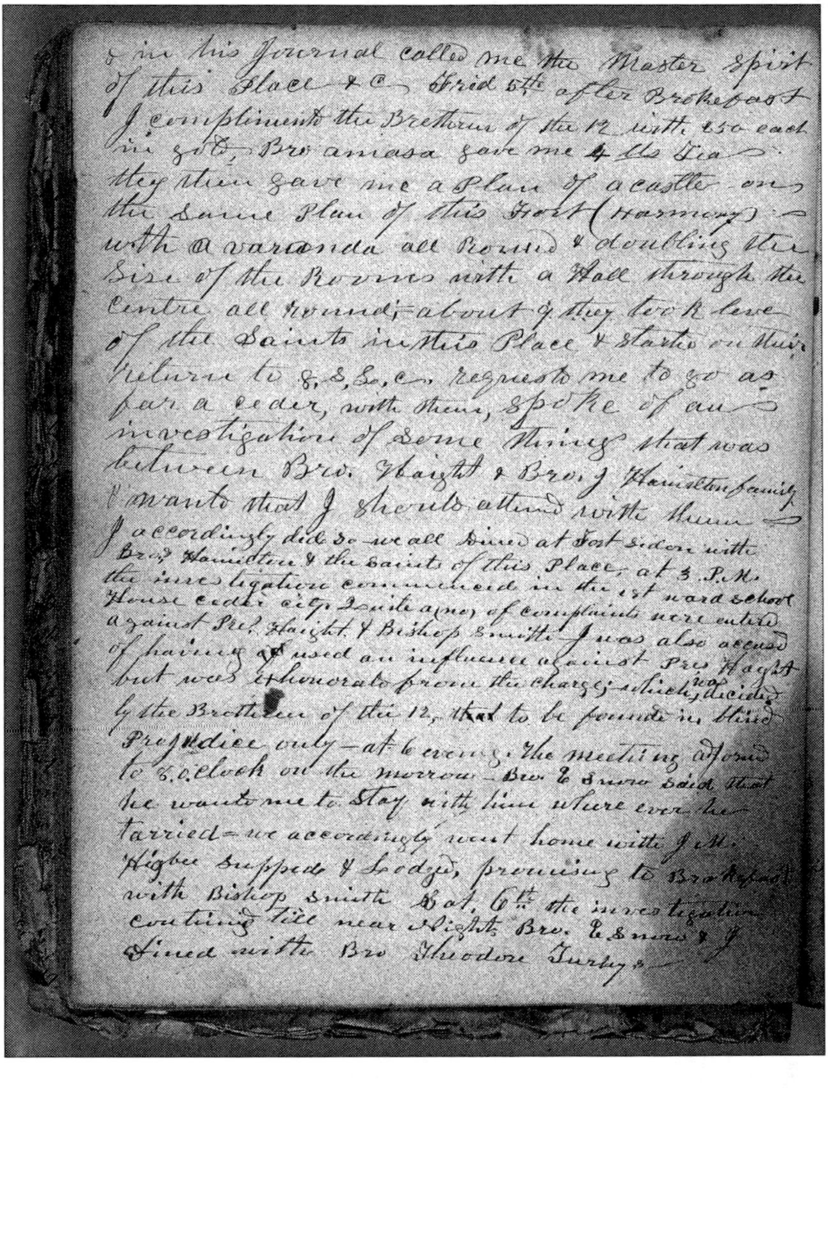

& in this Journal called me the Master Spirit
of this Place &c Frid 5th after Brekfast
I complimentd the Brethren of the 12 with $50 each
in gold, Bro Amasa gave me 4 lbs Tea
they then gave me a Plan of a castle on
the Same Plan of this Fort (Harmony)
with a varanda all Round & doubling the
Size of the Rooms with a Hall through the
Centre all round about & they took leave
of the Saints in this Place & started on their
return to G. S. L. C. requested me to go as
far as Ceder, with them, spoke of an
investigation of some things that was
between Bro. Haight & Bro. J. Hamilton family
& wanted that I should attend with them
I accordingly did so we all dined at Fort Sidon with
Bro. Hamilton & the Saints of this Place, at 3 P.M.
the investigation commenced in the 1st ward school
House Ceder City. Quite a no. of complaints were entered
against Prest. Haight & Bishop Smith. I was also accused
of having used an influence against Pres Haight
but was exhonorated from the charges which was decided
by the Brethren of the 12, that to be founded in blind
Prejudice only— at 6 eveng. the meeting adjourned
to 8 o'clock on the morrow— Bro E Snow said that
he wanted me to stay with him where ever he
tarried— we accordingly went home with J. M.
Higbee supped & Lodged, promising to Brekfast
with Bishop Smith Sat. 6th the investigation
continued till near Night. Bro. E Snow & I
dined with Bro Theodore Turley.

The Brethren of the (12.) heard the complaints of the Brethren
then reproved the authorities for the unwise policy which
they had adopted to govern the People & tole them that they
should never over rate their influence amoung the
People & then tole the People that they were at liberty to
remove to any Settlement where they thought that
they could better their condition—in turn reprove all
gave good counsel blessed & dismissed, I sent some
5$ dessert currency by the Brethren of 12. Made a present
of 15$ to Bro. E. Snow, took care of them & returned
home found my wife Emma Quite sick;
I will here Record a vision that I had a short time
ago— I was praying to the Lord, that I should not
fall into the hands of my Enimies, (as I had understood
that the U.S. officials had my Name & were determine to take me,) as I was thus Praying I was
caught up in the air some 20 feet high was I was
ascending 2 Dogs tryed to Ketch me by the feet
but failed; I was carried to the front of Prs B. youngs
Mansion & there remained until my Enimies were
all gone—then I came to the Earth again; soon a new
attempt was made but without success—I was again
caught up to the Top of Prs B. youngs Mansion where
I was out of the reach of my Enimies; some of
my wives were much troubled about me & feared
that I would suffer for food—; not knowing that
I was sustained from the rich Banquett of the Mansion
or Prs Table when my Enimies were gone I again

returned to the Earth; telling my Family all that
I had been in the vision; after this a group of People
presented themselves before me & insisted to have
me waft myself in the Air; having heard
that I had Power to do so, in opposition to this
spirit, I reluctantly assented to gratify their
wishes; the moment that I consented, the ad-
-vasary had Power over me, & when I was only 3
feet from the Earth, the spirit moved one
the right arm, which threw me off my
balance, I caught on my hands, 3 men of the P.Hood
seeing my situation ran to my assistance & help
me up right again & restored my arm — & thus
the vision came to a close; leaving me to marvel
at what I had seen.

Said aug. 7th I Preached to the Saints in fort Harmy
Mond 8th. I commence Harvesting my wheat
I had 30 acres tolerable crop, I also contract with
Bro. E. Morris & I Parry to Rough coat my Buildings
with Lime & gravel also to put a lime cement roof
on my Mansion all of which was warrant watter-
proof — the total Expence was about $600.
during this Month I contracted with Jacob
Workman, Cy Prep. Webster Staply, Jas
Davies & Darias Shirts to make me 15,000
adobies, for which I Paid 6$ Pr 1000, total
Cost is 70,50 &c up to Sept. 10th I was thra-
-shing & taking of my grain I also con-
-tracted with Richard Wooly & Hyrum to make
me 2,25 Rods of fence for a Pasture
at 3,25 &c a Rod — which amounts to the sum of

The preceding entries in the John D. Lee Journal cover the period from August 5
through September 14, 1868. The summary of the early days of September is dated
September 8. The next entry in the journal (not reproduced) is September 15. Note
the differing pens and the apparent insertions. Reproduced by permission of the
Huntington Library, San Marino, California.

This lack of information and the inconsistencies in the Lee, Arapeen, Armstrong, Haight, and Hamblin versions called for an additional investigation. After a visit to Cedar City on August 15, Lyman traveled to Beaver where he met with Smith, Rich, and Snow on August 18. On August 19, Smith continued northward, but Lyman, Rich, and Snow left for Cedar City and Harmony.[83]

On August 23, the three apostles went to Harmony; from there, they took Lee to Cedar City.[84] On the 23 and 24, they "held a council of inquiry in relation to many complaints made against" Haight and Klingensmith.[85] In a misdated entry, Lee wrote that he "was also accusd of having used an influence against Pres. Haight but was exhoneratd from the charge, which was decided by the Brethren of the 12, to be foundd in blind Prejudice only." Nevertheless, the three apostles reproved the stake president and bishop "for the un[w]ise policy which they had adopted to govern the People & told them that they should never over rate their influence amoung the People & then told the People that they were at liberty to remove to any settlement where they thought that they could better their condition."[86]

Although the hearing seemed to clear Lee of blame, the charges apparently worried him. Lee returned to Harmony "after dark" on August 25, from what Marion Jackson Shelton, a schoolteacher working for Lee, called "An inquisition held in Cedar City." On September 2, Shelton wrote that "Brother Lee has been very cross for several days past."[87] Lee's diary contains no entries for those days.

The minutes do not tell us just what the apostles learned at Parowan, and the only available information on the Cedar City hearings comes from Lee's misdated journal entries. On the basis of the available evidence, it seems likely that Smith and Lyman concluded at Parowan that Lee had used some influence with Haight that caused the stake president to send him out to gather the Paiutes to trail the emigrants. The hearings by Lyman, Snow, and Rich in Cedar City seem to have cleared Lee of influencing Haight, as the cryptic entry about charges and exoneration indicate. The apostles appeared to conclude, though, that the authority inherent in offices that Haight and Klingensmith held as church leaders led Lee and others to carry the attacks too far, eventually causing the massacre.

In the meantime, events in Salt Lake City influenced the investigation and prosecution of the massacre participants. We should understand that the federal officials who came on the heels of the Utah Expedition did not form a unified bloc. In the spring of 1859, a tense confrontation raged between two groups of federal officials. One group—Jacob Forney called them "Ultras"— consisted of the judges, U.S. marshal, and army officers. The other— we might call them moderates—included Governor Alfred Cumming, U.S. Attorney Alexander Wilson, and Forney.[88] The conflict reached a climax over Judge Cradlebaugh's use of the army to intimidate Provo citizens and imprison the mayor and other community leaders in the guard tent as he held court there in March and April 1859. Though the soldiers had to release the civic leaders for lack of evidence, these and other conflicts between townspeople and the soldiers led Cumming to appeal to Washington for authority to place the military under his control. Cumming's request led to orders from Attorney General Jeremiah Black, published in local papers on June 29, 1859, prohibiting judges from using the army for a civil process without the governor's approval.[89]

On April 2, 1859, Cradlebaugh had adjourned his court and returned with the army unit to Camp Floyd. On April 24, Young, Wells, and Smith met with Cumming and learned of his request to place the army under his control. A month later, reflecting on Cradlebaugh and the army, Brigham Young said he wanted both to bring the guilty to justice and to protect the Mormon community from persecution. On May 25, 1859, Young told George A. Smith that "so soon as the present excitement subsided, and the army could be kept from interfering with the Judiciary, he intended to have all the charges investigated . . . ." Young said he "would try to get the Governor & Dist. Atty. to go to Washington County, and manage the investigation of the Mountain Meadow Massacre, themselves."[90]

Earlier in May, Salt Lake County probate judge Elias Smith, a prominent Mormon, had initiated an investigation of the charges against Brigham Young. He issued a warrant for Young's arrest, charging him with sending written and verbal messages which led to the massacre. Young appeared voluntarily before Smith on May 12, 1859. Acknowledging the participation of "'armed [presumably white] men'" in the massacre, Smith specifically cited Cradlebaugh's charges that Young had instigated the murders. Young denied the charges, then demanded a "'fair and impartial'" investigation and trial. On the basis of Young's appearance and demands, Smith ordered county sheriff Robert T. Burton to arrest Young. Burton arrested Young, but as Will Bagley noted, the charges may have been dismissed because of lack of evidence.[91]

On June 18, 1859, Young met with George A. Smith and Jacob Hamblin and reiterated for Hamblin what he had told Smith the previous month about urging those accused to come forward to stand trial. If the federal judges would conduct the trials fairly without military interference, Young said, they should preside over the trials of the accused.[92] Reflecting, most probably, on his 1859 meeting with Cumming, Young said in a March 8, 1863, sermon that he had "told" the

> Governor . . . that if he would take an unprejudiced judge into the district where that horrid affair occurred, I would pledge myself that every man . . . should be forthcoming when called for, to be condemned or acquitted as an impartial, unprejudiced judge and jury should decide; and I pledged him that the court should be protected from any violence or hindrance in the prosecution of the laws; and if any were guilty of the blood of those who suffered in the Mountain Meadow massacre, let them suffer the penalty of the law.[93]

In a hearsay statement published after Cumming's death, an informant said that the governor had accused Young of lying to him, but in Young's view the judges then presiding, supported by military violence, hardly qualified as "unprejudiced."[94]

Young's 1863 statement occurred four years after the 1859 events, but documents from June and July 1859 show that in addition to demanding an investigation of his own culpability, Young and the church leadership paved a way to bring the massacre perpetrators to justice. On July 5, 1859, after the public knew that Cumming had received word from Washington placing the army under the governor's control, Young met with George A. Smith, Albert Carrington, and James Ferguson. They discussed the "reaction to the Mountain Meadow Massacre." Young told them that U.S. attorney Alexander Wilson had called "to consult with him about making some arrests of" the accused.[95]

On the same day, Wilson had met with Young. Young told him "that if the judges would open a court at Parowan or some other convenient location in the south, . . . unprejudiced and uninfluenced by . . . the army, so that man could have a fair and impartial trial He would go there himself, and he presumed that Gov. Cumming would also go . . . ." He "would use all his influence to have the parties arrested and have the whole . . . matter investigated thoroughly and impartially and justice meted out to every man." Young said he would not exert himself, however, "to arrest men to be treated like dogs and dragged about by the army, and confined and abused by them," presumably referring to the actions of Cradlebaugh and the army in Provo. Young said that if the judges and army treated people that way, the federal officials "must hunt them up themselves."[96]

Wilson agreed that it was unfair "to drag men and their witnesses 200 or 300 miles to trial." Young said "the people wanted a fair and impartial court of justice, like they have in other states and territories, and if he had anything to do with it, the army must keep its place." Wilson said he felt "the proposition was reasonable and he would propose it to the judges."[97]

Now confident that the army would not intrude and abuse or murder Mormons, and that the U.S. attorney and governor would support them, the church leaders lent their influence to bringing the accused into court. On June 15, 1859, to prepare the way for the administration of justice, Brigham Young had told George A. Smith and Jacob Hamblin that "as soon as a Court of Justice could be held, so that men could be heard without the influence of the military he should advise men accused to come forward and demand trial on the charges preferred against them for the Mountain Meadow Massacre" as he had previously done. Then he again sent George A. Smith and Amasa Lyman south, this time to urge those accused of the crime to prepare for trial and to try to suppress Mormon-authored crime.[98] The leaders had grown sufficiently troubled over the mounting evidence of some crimes that they also moved to release the suspects from leadership positions and to chastise the overzealous throughout the territory for condoning violence and theft based on their misunderstanding of church doctrine.

In 1859, Young, Lyman and Smith elaborated on doctrine emphasizing peace and brotherly love, in the spirit of the change in the Mormon Reformation of 1856 and 1857 authored by Wilford Woodruff beginning in early December 1856. Following the death of Jedediah Grant in December 1856, Woodruff, with Young's apparent approval, contradicted the violent aspects of previous hyperbole about blood atonement. In the cover letter to officials sent with the proclamation of martial law in September 1857, Young and Wells admonished the leaders to "let all things be done peacefully but with firmness and let there be no excitement."[99] In a similar vein, on March 14, 15, 16, and 17, 1859, Apostle Amasa Lyman preached in Washington, Santa Clara, and Harmony, with Lee, Haight, John M. Higbee, and Charles Hopkins in the audience, that "Shedding of Blood . . . was not right," and "killing is not an ordinance of the gospel."[100] We do not avenge "the blood of the Prophets . . . by Butchering" others, but rather "by implanting in the mind & cultivating the opposite principle."[101]

Hearing the message at least three times, Lee missed or ignored its substance when he described it as "an interesting discource on the Subject of avenging the Blood of the Prophets."[102]

Echoing Lyman's sentiments in a speech in the Tabernacle on May 22, 1859, Young said that although he was "accused of having great influence" with his people, "he would to God that he had influence sufficient to make every man that calls himself a Saint do right." Praising the American government, Young also spent time "admonishing the Saints to be faithful and patient and not to take judgment into their own hands, and by the help of the Lord, he would lead them to the fountain of light."[103]

Elaborating on these messages, Smith and Lyman, on the way south in early July, visited various settlements in which they attempted to "learn the spirit of the people" and to tailor their talks to local needs. On July 10 at Mount Pleasant, where, Smith said, the "spirit manifested tended to rowdyism, we preached to them upon the subject . . . ."[104] In a speech in Manti on July 13, Smith declared that in the face of the efforts of the government "to exterminate the Mormons," that "the worst thing" for the Church "was the intemperance of some Elders," particularly "some who desired to Steal from U.S. property."[105] Amasa Lyman denounced in no uncertain terms murder, blood atonement, and the stealing of gentile property. He said that "we had to cultivate virtue and love for each" other. The Saints, he said, should not try to become "the ministers of death; it was only a Barbarians Spirit to have blood for blood."[106] In Parowan, on July 17, 1859 after Smith and Lyman had preached, Dame "called on all to keep the laws of the land as well as those of the church . . . ." Civil authorities, he said, should "suppress all fighting and other disturbances."[107]

Smith and Lyman continued on their tour south, preaching in settlements along their route.[108] On July 22 and 23, they both preached in Harmony, and again, Lee failed to understand the intended message.[109] On July 25, Smith and Lyman "warn[ed] the Saints of associating with reckless characters" and "organized bands of thieves."[110]

The following Sunday, July 31, Smith and Lyman shook up the leadership of the church in Cedar City. Smith "disorganized the Stake," releasing Philip Klingensmith, Samuel McMurdy, and John Morris from the bishopric and Isaac Haight, John Higbee, and Elias Morris from the stake presidency.[111] In their place, he called Henry Lunt, Richard Morris, and Thomas Jones, none of whom had participated in the massacre, as a combined bishopric-stake presidency.[112]

Cedar City's plummeting population "undoubtedly [contributed to] the decision to combine normally separate offices into one."[113] The massacre also contributed.[114] Haight said he asked for a release because he expected to be hiding out: "In consequence of the persecution of our enemies."[115] Klingensmith had, however, not asked for a release, and all except perhaps John Morris had planned or participated in the massacre.

The apostles apparently told the massacre leaders to prepare for trial. The next day, as Smith and Lyman traveled northward, Klingensmith wrote to Smith, asking him and Hosea Stout to defend him in the forthcoming "proceedings . . . against me in a case of alleged murder at the Mountain Meadows," sending a deed to his property in Cedar City as a retainer.[116] A few days later, Lyman met with Lee on "special business;" and again proclaiming his innocence, Lee also wrote asking Smith and Stout to defend him if he were arrested "upon the charge of aiding in the Massacre at the Meadows."[117] Most significantly, after these events, on September 11, 1859, Lee confided to his journal, that the perpetrators could expect "neither Sucor, Simpany, or Pity" from the church leadership in evading lawful prosecution.[118]

George A. Smith confirmed Lee's judgment in a letter to Isaac Haight on November 6, 1859. Haight had sent a letter on October 17, transferring half ownership of his woollen factory as a retainer, and asking Smith to serve as his attorney. Maintaining the Church's position that the government should conduct trials without military assistance, he said that "it is policy for those accused to make the necessary arrangements for defence and should military despotism not succeed be prepared for the first opportunity to exonerate themselves before an impartial tribunal."[119]

During the summer of 1859, as Smith and Lyman shook up the massacre participants in southern Utah, Mormon leaders in northern Utah worked futilely to induce federal officials to accept their help in bringing the massacre perpetrators to justice. On August 6, 1859, U.S. attorney Wilson asked Marshal Dotson to deputize Territorial Marshal John Kay to arrest massacre suspects in southern Utah. Wilson said Kay "was a Mormon, had a knowledge of the country and of the people, and expressed a determination, if legally deputized, to make arrests if possible." Wilson pointed out that Brigham Young had promised to cooperate. Dotson, however, refused "to appoint Kay his deputy," because Kay "was a Morm[o]n."[120] Wilson asked Utah Chief Justice Delana R. Eckels to intercede with Dotson, but Eckels refused since Kay was "a notorious Mormon." To Eckels, accepting the church's help was acknowledging its power. "I never will acknowledge . . . ," he wrote, "a power . . . above the law."[121]

To make matters worse, instead of holding court in Parowan or Cedar City where Dotson and Wilson might have brought in participants and witnesses, Eckels opened court far to the north, in Nephi, on August 22.[122] Eckels assembled most of his grand jurors from among men from Camp Floyd, claiming that citizens of Utah County had fled before him.[123] Although some had fled, Utah County included Provo, the territory's second largest city, where he could easily have obtained jurors. Wilson sent Stephen DeWolfe, who later, as editor of the *Valley Tan*, showed himself a bitter anti-Mormon, to Nephi as prosecuting attorney.[124]

Yet, with a stacked jury and an anti-Mormon prosecutor, Eckels could obtain neither indictments against nor convictions of massacre participants. He complained of inadequate funding.[125] He neglected to mention that William Hooper had offered $1,500 to defer court expenses, and Brigham Young and John Kay had offered to help the U.S. marshal and protect the court as a public service. DeWolfe, however, cited the main barrier to success when he pointed out the distance between Nephi and the settlements south of Parowan, "and the difficulty, if not impossibility, of bringing . . .[witnesses] before the court [in faraway Nephi] in any reasonable time."[126] Wilson agreed, and Cumming scolded the judges for their obsession with hounding "the leading men of the Mormon Church."[127] Citing a list of those he believed most guilty—all from southern Utah—Forney complained of the judges' inaction and of the stupidity of the judges in publicly naming the suspects before trying to "catch them" and refusing the help of Young, Kay, or Hooper.[128]

Significantly, Eckels's prejudices did not signal the end of Brigham Young's willingness to bring the Mountain Meadows killers to justice. On September 2, Young met with Hooper who was about to depart for Washington. He told Hooper that if someone asked him "why he had not brought the guilty parties to justice," he should answer that "if law and justice could take place no one could be more willing than he would be."[129] Echoing these sentiments, the *Deseret News* attacked the federal judges for talking tough but refusing to act.[130]

Eckels, however, reiterated his scorn for Mormon help. Writing to Secretary of State Lewis Cass, he defended his decision to hold court in Nephi instead of southern Utah, attacked the moderate federal officials, and asked again for army support. In spite of Young's attempt to help, he wrote that he believed a competent attorney "could show that Brigham Young directed the Mountain Meadow Massacre . . . ."[131]

To check out Eckels's complaints, Cass sent a copy of Eckels's letter to Cumming, asking his opinion on the matter. The governor replied that contrary to anti-Mormon propaganda, he believed "Person's unbiased by prejudice" would agree that they had "seldom seen" a community "more marked by quiet and peaceable diligence, than that of the Mormons." He blamed rather the "hundreds of adventurers" who accompanied the army for local violence and theft.[132]

By 1860, then, the church leadership knew that the story that Lee had told Young and Woodruff in 1857 was untrue. Apparently, however, the church leaders did not yet know of the large number of militiamen involved in the massacre, and they may still have believed that Indians under the supervision of Lee and a few others had carried it out. Significantly, they probably did not know that many of the white men who participated did so under church and military duress. Summarizing his understanding of murders committed in the territory, Young in May 1860 wrote in response to an inquiry from his friend Hiram McKee, a Protestant minister he had known since his early days in New York, that the whole was "far more repugnant to my feelings than I suppose it can be to yours." He stated further that "Indians and wicked [white] men," had committed the murders, though this may have been a general comment on violence rather than a specific comment on the massacre.[133]

Moreover, as late as 1861, Young still believed the stories of Baker-Fancher crimes which led to the massacre, in spite of his efforts to bring the perpetrators to trial. On visiting the massacre site in May 1861, Woodruff recorded Young's assessment that the plaque Carleton had erected on the mass grave which read: "Vengeance is mine and I will repay saith the Lord," should read: "Vengence is mine and I [the Lord] have taken a little."[134] Young clearly refused to take responsibility for the massacre. Later, the same month, Young told John D. Lee that the emigrants "Meritd their fate, & the only thing that ever troubled him was the lives of the Women & children, but that under the circumstances [this] could not be avoided."[135]

The outbreak of the Civil War in 1861 slowed the investigation of the massacre. In 1863, however, Young again urged the government to bring the perpetrators to justice. He reminded an audience of his promise to Governor Cumming that if those accused were brought to trial before "an impartial, unprejudiced judge and jury," he would do all he could to protect the court and allow the guilty to "suffer the penalty of the law." The offer, he said, "still held."[136]

Significantly, however, Young and the leadership still believed that the principal culpability lay with John D. Lee. In April 1863, after the general conference, Young; his first counselor, Heber C. Kimball; and apostles George A. Smith and Orson Hyde headed south with a large party.[137] On May 6, 1863, they visited Lee in Washington and Young condemned him before the apostles and others present. Recording the event, David John wrote: "Young spoke to . . . [Lee] about the 'Mountain Meadow'. . . , [Lee] tried to blame the Indians for the massacre, but Pres Young, would not accept his testimony, and at last said, 'John D. Lee, do all the good you can, while you live, and you shall be credited, with every good deed you perform, but, where God and the Lamb dwell, you shall never be.' Lee, wept bitterly."[138] Although the General Authorities did not officially excommunicate him until 1870, Lee himself reportedly said that in 1863 he considered himself cut off from the church.[139]

We do not know what led to Young's 1863 denunciation of Lee, but we do know that Apostle Erastus Snow, by then the principal leader in the southern Utah colonies, had undertaken an investigation of the massacre. He had undoubtedly learned various facts during the 1858 hearings in Cedar City. Moreover, as he later wrote, "After colonies of our people began to locate in Washington County," he "began to learn that . . . Lee had taken a direct hand with the Indians in that affair; and I felt it my duty to acquaint the Presidency of the Church with the facts so far as I had been able to gather them." He enlisted the help of Bishop Lorenzo W. Roundy of Kanarra.[140] Snow attended the church's general conference in Salt Lake City in April 1863, and he may have communicated what he had learned to Young.[141]

By the mid-1860s, since federal officials still refused to accept his assistance in apprehending and prosecuting the perpetrators, Young expected them to bring the guilty to justice without him. On May 8, 1866, in a conversation with several military officers, Young said that he had "urged, from the days of Governor Cumming . . . for Judges from the First Judicial District to go south and investigate" the massacre and "pledged . . . to protect them with my life in so doing but they would not do it." He believed that they really did not want to investigate because by leaving "the matter in an unsettled condition," they could "reflect evil on me . . . ." He said that "if there were Mormons guilty in that act . . . let them be brought to justice."[142]

Addressing a congregation in the Salt Lake Tabernacle on December 23, 1866, Young urged the authorities not to "cease their efforts until you find the murderers."[143] In 1869, he again reminded George Hicks of his offer to Governor Cumming, adding that he had made it "again and again," and concluding "God will judge this matter and on that assurance I rest perfectly satisfied."[144]

In spite of their disaffection from Lee, both Erastus Snow and Brigham Young interacted civilly on business and church matters with him till 1870 and on business thereafter down to 1874 when Deputy Marshal William Stokes finally captured him.[145]

In contrast to Brigham Young's open statements that white men had been involved in the massacre, George A. Smith was less than forthright. As late as the fall of 1869, in responding to reporters' questions, he still attributed the massacre to Indians, though he admitted whites were there, "but arrived too late" to prevent the tragedy.[146] Truthfully, however, Smith explained that Young and his associates were always "ready to give every aid in their power to discover and bring to Justice the participants in this massacre."[147]

By 1870, the major participants were often away from southwestern Utah. Under Young's urging, Lee, with extreme reluctance, settled for a time at Skutumpah northeast of Kanab and then at Lee's Ferry and Moenave in northern Arizona.[148] Haight, Higbee, William Stewart, and George Adair lived and worked in southern Utah and northern Arizona. Klingensmith moved to Nevada and eventually turned state's evidence against Lee.

Although federal officials spurned church assistance, Erastus Snow continued to gather information with the help of Bishop Lorenzo Roundy of Kanarra. Snow later testified that he and Roundy "communicated to President Young the facts as we had learned them, and the sources of our information."[149] Meeting with Young in 1870, Roundy said that the president "did not know the truth" and told him he had "been misled and deceived." "If you want to know the truth," Roundy said, "ask Nephi Johnson . . . ." After meeting with Johnson in Kanarra, Young "expressed great astonishment, and said if such were the facts, Lee had added to his crime lying and deceit."[150]

Young's party traveled north to Cedar City, and the following morning he spoke at the meetinghouse.[151] Afterward, Young asked his nephew, John R. Young to walk with him. They met Lee, who, according to John R., "reached out his hand, to shake hands." Brigham Young refused and said,

"'John what made you lie to me about the Mountain Meadow Massacre?'" Lee refused to answer. President Young bristled and told Lee never to "come again into my presence" or to seek to be "Refellowshiped into the Church . . . ."[152]

Johnson's memory of the events differed from John Young's version. He dated the conversation in Salt Lake City "fifteen or twenty years" after the massacre rather than in Kanarra, while John Young placed the events in 1865. Johnson said that as he spoke, Young "walked the floor, . . . and several times said why did Lee lie to me . . . ." Johnson said that he told Young that most of the men were young, went under orders, and believed "when they left Cedar City, that the emigrants had been killed by the Indians . . . [and they] were going to bury the dead, . . . they took their shovels along, and their arms to protect themselves" from possible Indian attack. These were reminiscent accounts, and both men appear to have been confused about the date of Lee's excommunication.[153]

What could Brigham Young have learned from Nephi Johnson in 1870 that he did not know before? The evidence suggests that he learned that some who took part in the massacre did so under the false assumptions. Some thought they were going to save the emigrants from the Indians. Others believed they were going to help bury the dead from an Indian massacre. Still others, like Johnson, went under church and military duress. Young told Johnson he would not hold the men who were forced to go responsible, "but . . . .he would hold . . . [the leaders] respon[s]ible."[154] Significantly, this was the same position that both Judge Jacob Boreman and the anti-Mormon *Salt Lake Tribune* took on the question.

Brigham Young's company reached Salt Lake on September 24, 1870, and on October 8 between conference sessions, Young called a "council" of the Twelve Apostles.[155] After laying "the facts before them," Young "proposed, and all present unanimously voted to expel John D. Lee and Isaac C. Haight, who was his superior officer in the Church, for failing to restrain him, and to take prompt action against him." Snow said Young instructed that "Lee should, under no circumstances, ever be again admitted as a member of the Church." Wilford Woodruff said that the same applied to Haight.[156]

When Lee learned that the Twelve had excommunicated him and Haight, he accepted it stoically, though he professed not to know the reason. He later became disturbed as the excommunication disrupted his family and turned people against him.[157] He reported various dreams, one in which he tried to clean a dirty, half-naked Erastus Snow.[158] In another, he concluded that Young had acted to punish him for a short time to deflect persecution from apostates.[159] Juanita Brooks believed that the excommunications took place then because "sentiment from within the church became so strong that by 1870 the leaders were forced" to act.[160] Will Bagley thought the church leaders picked Lee as a scapegoat because they believed he would take it like a man and that his excommunication would deflect attention from the church leaders.[161]

The disruption of his family led Lee to try to patch things up between himself and Young. Driving to St. George on December 22, 1870, he asked Young why he should be cut off thirteen years after the massacre. Young told him that he had not learned the "particuelars until lately."[162] Instead of blaming the Paiutes as he had in 1857, Lee insisted to Young that he had told the president "the whole Truth . . . with the Exception of one thing." That "one thing" was that he "suffered the blame to rest on" himself. Instead, he told Young, he should have told of the others who were present and pointed out that "what we done was by the mutual consent" of church leaders after prayer. "Righteousness alone prompted the act," he insisted.[163] After Lee begged him, Young agreed to give him a rehearing, sending him to Erastus Snow to arrange it.[164] Snow, however, who knew many facts in the case, refused to hold the rehearing, arguing "it would result in no benefit."[165]

Though upset at the refusal, within a few days, Lee thought that there would be "Justice in the rulers of Iseral [sic] yet," probably thinking Young would forgive him.[166] Haight, who lived in Toquerville at the time, felt much differently. He said that "he feared he would never get a hearing until" the church got a new president.[167] As confident as he was of forgiveness, Lee blamed both Snow and Roundy for his excommunication. On January 3, 1871 at a party in Kanarra, Lee responded with anger to Roundy's friendly greeting. Accusing Roundy of trying to poison "the Mind of" Brigham Young "in an Evil hour," he confronted the bishop with: "Every Dog will have his day, . . . Now is your day. By & by it will be my day."[168]

Significantly, in spite of Lee's optimism and Haight's pessimism, Haight was the one who managed to get his ban lifted. In February, 1874, the new Toquerville bishop, William A. Bringhurst, spoke with Young about Haight's membership. Young replied, "Isaac Haight will be damned in this world and will be damned throughout eternity."[169] In spite of this, Haight's defenders—particularly a son-in-law—persuaded Young that he had "misunderstood" Haight's role in the massacre.[170] On March 3, 1874 Haight was rebaptized into the church and his blessings were restored.[171]

What was this so-called "misunderstanding?" In writing about the affair, B. H. Roberts said, "Some mitigating circumstances subsequently were learned respecting Haight's responsibilities in the matter of not restraining Lee, and he was restored to church fellowship."[172] Apparently, Haight's defenders were able to convince Young that since he was not actually on the ground at the massacre, his only culpability was in his inability to restrain Lee.

In 1872, Young wrote to the War Department and reiterated the offer he had made to Cumming in 1858. Still fearful of army violence, he argued at the same time against the establishment of Fort Cameron in the south. He wrote that "sending an armed force is not the best means of furthering the ends of justice, although it may serve an excellent purpose, in exciting popular clamor against the 'Mormons.'" He said that he feared that the motive for the fort was to stir conflict between soldiers and settlers, rather than to protect the people from Indian raids, since Beaver was a poor place to meet that need. He argued that Cradlebaugh and Eckels "accomplished absolutely nothing" in prosecuting the massacre because—at least in Cradlebaugh's case, "instead of honoring the law, . . .[he] took a course to screen offenders, who could easily hide from such a posse under the justification of avoiding a trial by court martial."[173] Now, he wrote, after fourteen years, instead of trying "to prosecute the accused . . . some of the Judges, like Judge [Cyrus] Hawley, have used every opportunity to charge the crime upon prominent men in Utah, and inflame public opinion against our community."[174]

On April 5, 1874, Lee had his last visit with Brigham Young. He said that he found Young outwardly cordial.[175] By contrast, Young said that he berated Lee, urging him if had killed the emigrants to "hang yourself."[176] Since Lee's account was written at the time and Young's later, I believe that Lee was accurate.

Federal marshals subsequently arrested Lee, Dame, Ellott Willden, Philip Klingensmith, and George Adair, but the U.S. attorney could not gather enough evidence to prosecute Dame, Wilden, and Adair. The U.S. marshals who had the duty to capture the others who were indicted were unable to do so, so none of them stood trial. Klingensmith turned state's evidence in Lee's first trial but did not testify in the second. As Lee wrote in 1859, "Catching is before hanging."[177]

Young and Smith both made statements about the massacre in depositions that the prosecution introduced, and, at Lee's insistence, the defense admitted them in his trial. The depositions in which both declared themselves innocent of the massacre, seem to be essentially accurate except that Brigham Young through George A. Smith counseled the settlers not to sell grain or to trade with the emigrants rather than simply telling them not to sell grain for animal fodder, as the depositions stated.[178]

Currently available evidence does not allow us to know just when or understand how much general church leaders knew about responsibility for the massacre before 1870, when they clearly knew nearly everything. It seems apparent, however, that they gained complete knowledge over a rather lengthy time. From Jacob Hamblin's and George A. Smith's 1858 reports, they knew that John D. Lee and other militiamen participated in some way; perhaps they believed the militiamen had led the massacre. With this knowledge in 1859 Young and his associates, William H. Hooper and Territorial Marshal John Kay, offered assistance to the federal attorney, marshal, and judges. The marshal and judge rejected that assistance. Young continued to renew that offer during the 1860s and early 1870s, and the federal officials continued to ignore it.

By 1863, Young apparently learned more, and he distanced himself from Lee. Between 1863 and 1870, however, he seems to have mellowed toward Lee. By 1870, the investigation by Erastus Snow and Lorenzo Roundy had revealed the culpability of both Lee and Haight. It seems probable, though, that it was not until Young's 1870 conversation with Nephi Johnson that he understood that the local leaders had lied to some men in the community by telling them they were going to bury the victims of an Indian massacre. It is also not clear that the general authorities understood the large number of men involved in the massacre. They may have taken some time to learn that the leaders had forced the euro-American men under military and local church discipline to murder innocent people.

Significantly, contrary to the usual stories that interpret Young's role either as the author of the massacre or as refusing to investigate it or as erecting a stonewall against the investigation, it is abundantly clear that federal officials, not Brigham Young, were responsible for stonewalling. Their motive, evident from frequent statements by federal judges and apostates who accused Young of planning the massacre, seems to have resulted from a futile attempt to muster enough evidence to indict President Young himself. As late as 1875, this seems evident in the way Robert Baskin prosecuted Lee in his first trial. His prosecution was either incompetent or cleverly aimed at swaying public opinion against Young and the Mormon leadership.[179] Nevertheless, Young and others in the church leadership not only investigated the massacre and advised the participants to prepare for trial as early as 1859, they also meted out some punishment, including releases from positions of authority and, ultimately, the excommunications of Lee and Haight. Klingensmith, too, was apparently excommunicated, but we do not have the records to determine when and why.

Could the church leaders have done more to bring the perpetrators to justice? Almost certainly. Until the decision in Ferris v. Higley in 1874 that limited their jurisdiction, the church leadership could have forced the prosecution in the local probate courts. Under the circumstances, though, the accused might have taken their convictions to the U.S. Supreme Court and obtained a similar decision earlier. Moreover, Eckels and other judges believed the probate courts illegal, and when Eckels found prisoners "arrested by the local authorities he invariably made the utmost exertion to set them at liberty." Given his prejudices, he might have interfered until the marshal and attorney had sufficient evidence to indict Brigham Young.[180] Still, we should understand the reluctance of Latter-day Saint officials during 1858 and early 1859 resulted principally from fear of army violence against the Mormon community. After June 1859, when they learned that the federal government had placed the army under civilian control, the Church leaders attempted to cooperate with federal officials, but the officials refused to accept the cooperation.

For some reason, Haight's supporters convinced Young, falsely I believe, that his only sin was his failure to control Lee. As a result, Young reinstated him, while he left Lee dangling. My own conclusion is that if anyone deserved excommunication and execution it was most certainly Isaac C. Haight. After all, the bulk of the murders had been committed by militiamen on his orders. Other culpable figures like John M. Higbee, Joel White, and William Stewart should have faced justice. In addition, Dame, while Haight may have deceived him initially, probably obstructed justice after the fact. Lee was a zealot to be sure, but he made a mess which other white men helped resolve—many under duress—in a brutal and tragic massacre while under orders from his church superior, Isaac Haight. In the final analysis, Young's investigations led to the wrong conclusion about Haight.

If anyone deserves the credit for investigating the massacre it was Erastus Snow. Juanita Brooks was right, Snow persevered because he found the work of building the kingdom in southwestern Utah hampered by the rumors circulating about the massacre and the role that church members—especially Lee and Haight—had played in it. Lee himself understood the central role Snow and Roundy played in clarifying the matter for Young, as shown by his dream about Snow and his confrontation with Roundy.

NOTES

1. Brigham Young, *Diary of Brigham Young, 1857,* ed. Everett L. Cooley (Salt Lake City: Tanner Trust Fund, University of Utah Library, 1980), 50–51.
2. Young, *Diary,* 17, 18, 21, 24, 26, 28–29, 38, 62 (June 9, 10, 14, 19, 21, and 23; July 6; and August 20, 1857).
3. Young, *Diary,* 42 (July 12, 1857).
4. Young, *Diary,* 48–49 (July 24, 1857).
5. The term "theo-democracy" comes from John W. Gunnison, *The Mormons, or Latter-Day Saints, in the Valley of the Great Salt Lake . . .* (Philadelphia: Lippincott, 1860; repr., Brookline, MA: Paradigm, 1993), v, cited in Ronald W. Walker, David J. Whittaker, and James B. Allen, *Mormon History* (Urbana: University of Illinois Press, 2001), 10.
6. On this matter, the best source is probably Wilford Woodruff, *Wilford Woodruff's Journal, 1833–1898,* ed. Scott G. Kenney, 9 vols. (Midvale, Utah: Signature Books, 1983–1985). For a scholarly discussion of the operation of councils in the nineteenth-century LDS Church, see Kathleen Flake, "From Conferences to Councils: The Development of LDS Church Organization, 1830–1835," *Archive of Restoration Culture: Summer Fellows' Papers, 1997–1999* (Provo, UT: Joseph Fielding Smith Institute for Latter-day Saint History, 2000), 1–8; for a modern interpretation of the functioning of LDS Church leadership through councils, see M. Russell Ballard, *Counseling with Our Councils: Learning to Minister Together in the Church and in the Family* (Salt Lake City: Deseret Book, 1997).
7. The most evident examples of resistance took place during the Walker War with Ute Indians of the early 1850s and the attempt to organize communitarian United Orders in the 1850s and early 1870s. In both periods, members resisted centrally administered policies.
8. Young, *Diary,* 54, 55, 56, 57, 58, 59, 60, 61: July 27 (got information), July 31 (discussed information), Aug. 1 (decided to start own mail service), Aug. 4 (addressed recalling Saints), Aug. 5 (discussed starting express company), Aug. 8 (discussed recalling Saints), Aug. 9 (met about government actions), Aug. 11 (decided to vacate Fort Supply), Aug. 12 (called home European missionaries), Aug. 13 (met with advisors and called out militia), Aug. 15 (called home Carson Valley Saints), Aug. 16 (reviewed preparing to defend church through evacuation if necessary), and Aug. 17 (considered actions of the army), 1857.
9. Young *Diary,* 36–37, 40, 47 (July 5, 10, and 19, 1857). On problems with Utah surveys see Thomas G. Alexander, *A Clash of Interests: Interior Department and Mountain West, 1863–1896* (Provo, UT: Brigham Young University Press, 1977), 7–8, 35. In 1874, Utah's U. S. surveyor general, Nathan Kimball, found earlier surveys "so conflicting and irregular as to require resurveys at an additional cost to the Government," p. 35.
10. Young, *Diary,* 62.
11. On this topic, the best source is probably Armand L. Mauss, *All Abraham's Children: Changing Mormon Conceptions of Race and Lineage,* (Urbana: University of Illinois Press, 2003), 41–73.
12. Woodruff, *Journal,* 5:88 (September 1, 1857). Dimick B. Huntington Journal, 1857–1859, September 1, 1857, MS d 1419, v. 2, Library and Archives of the Church of Jesus Christ of Latter-day Saints, Family and Church History Department, Church of Jesus Christ of Latter-day Saints, Salt Lake City, Utah (hereinafter LDS Archives).
13. Huntington Journal, September 1, 1858.
14. See particularly their success in taking cattle from the Turner-Dukes company, which followed the Baker-Fancher company that was attacked at Mountain Meadows.

15.   Brigham Young to James W. Denver, September 12, 1857, House Executive Document 71, 35th Cong., 1st Sess., 184–85, Serial 956.

16.   On supplying lumber see Woodruff, *Journal*, 5:91 (September 9, 1857). On his fear and disdain for the army see 5:92–93 (September 12, 1857).

17.   "A Statement by Jacob Hamblin given at Kanab, Nov 18th 1871" (hereinafter cited as Hamblin Statement, 1871), copy, LDS Church Archives.

18.   Hamblin Statement, 1871; Jacob Hamblin to Brigham Young, November 13, 1871, General Office Files, President Office Files, Brigham Young Office Files, box 74, fd. 19, LDS Church Archives.

19.   Will Bagley, *Blood of the Prophets: Brigham Young and the Mountain Meadows Massacre* (Norman: University of Oklahoma Press), 227; James Henry Carleton, *Report on the Subject of the Massacre at the Mountain Meadows, in Utah Territory, in September, 1857, of One Hundred and Twenty Men, Women and Children, Who Were from Arkansas* (Little Rock, Ark.: True Democrat Steam Press Print, 1860), 19–20; John Cradlebaugh, "Utah and the Mormons: speech of Hon. John Cradlebaugh, of Nevada, on the admission of Utah as a state, delivered in the House of Representatives, February 7, 1863," U.S. Congress, *Congressional Globe*, 37th Cong., 3rd Sess., Appendix, vol. 133: 122–23.

20.   William H. Rogers, "The Mountain Meadows Massacre, Statement of Mr. Wm. H. Rogers" *Valley Tan* 2 (February 29, 1860).

21.   Brigham Young to William H. Hooper, February 21, 1866, Brigham Young Letterpress Copybook 8:131, Brigham Young Office Files, LDS Church Archives.

22.   For the contrary view see Bagley, *Blood of the Prophets,* 137.

23.   Woodruff, *Journal*, 5:96 (September 13, 1857).

24.   Brigham Young to Jeter Clinton (Philadelphia), September 12, 1857; Young to William I. Appleby (New York), September 12, 1857; and Young to Orson Pratt (Liverpool), September 12, 1857, Letters Sent, Brigham Young Papers, LDS Church Archives.

25.   Woodruff, *Journal*, 5:98 (September 14, 1857); Brigham Young and Daniel H. Wells to William H. Dame, September 14, 1857, Letters Sent, Brigham Young Papers, LDS Church Archives.

26.   Huntington Journal, September 20, 1857.

27.   Historian's Office, Journal, 28 September 1857, p. 56, CR 100, 1, LDS Church Archives. Special thanks to Christy Best for identifying Hawkins's handwriting.

28.   Woodruff, *Journal,* 5:102–3 (September 29, 1857).

29.   Brigham Young Office Files, 1832–1878, September 29, 1857 (bulk 1844–1877), box 72, fd. 1, LDS Church Archives.

30.   John D. Lee, *A Mormon Chronicle, Chronicle: The Diaries of John D. Lee, 1848–1876,* ed. Robert Glass Cleland and Juanita Brooks, 2 vols. (San Marino, CA: Huntington Library, 1955), 2:152 (December 1870). The dates in Lee's journal are off. Lee dates this the twenty-ninth, but he says that it is Thursday, which would be the twenty-second; also the next entry is dated the Sunday the twenty-third. Cleland and Brooks correct it to the twenty-fifth. W. W. Bishop, ed., John D. Lee, *Mormonism Unveiled; Including the Remarkable Life and Confessions of the Late Mormon Bishop, John D. Lee . . . ."* (Albuquerque, NM.: Fierra Blanca Publication, 2001), 232. Lee or Bishop wrote (p. 258) that Lee had talked with Brigham Young, and no one else, when, in fact, he had reported to Young and Wilford Woodruff together. Woodruff, *Journal*, 5:102–3 (29 September 1857).

31.   Lee, *Mormon Chronicle*, 2:152 (29 December 1870). Note: the date numbering may be faulty.

32   Wilford Woodruff, "Affidavit of W. Woodruff," 1882, MS 2674, fd. 12, LDS Church Archives.

33.   Bishop, ed. *Mormonism Unveiled,* 254; Lee, *Mormon Chronicle,* 1:199; 214; 2:100–101.

34.   Abraham H. Cannon, *An Apostle's Record: The Journals of Abraham H. Cannon,* ed. Dennis B. Horne (Clearfield, UT: Gnolaum books, 2004), 408 (June 13, 1895).

35.   George W. Armstrong to Brigham Young, 30 September 1857, Bureau of Indian Affairs, Utah Superintendency Papers, RG 75, National Archives and Records Service, Washington D.C. in Juanita Brooks, *Mountain Meadows Massacre* (second ed., Norman: University of Oklahoma Press, 1962), 143.

36. John D. Lee to Brigham Young, November 20, 1857, quoted in Bishop, ed., *Mormonism Unveiled,* 260–61.
37. Brigham Young to William I. Cox, December 4, 1857, Letters Sent, Brigham Young Papers, LDS Church Archives; Brigham Young to James W. Denver, January 6, 1858, in Brigham Young Office Files, 1832–1878 (bulk 1844–1877) CR 1234, box 55, fd. 4, LDS Church Archives.
38. Brigham Young to William I. Cox, December 4, 1857; Young to Cox, November 5, 1857; and Young to Cox and William I. Crosby, October 1, 1857, Letters Sent, Brigham Young Papers, LDS Archives.
39. Garland Hurt to Jacob Forney, December 4, 1857, in "The Utah Expedition," U. S. Cong., House Executive Document 71, 35th Cong., 1st. Sess., 202–3, Serial 956.
40. Forney listed Isaac Haight, John D. Lee, Philip Klingensmith, John M. Higbee, David Tullis, Carl Shirts, "——— Thornley, Painter creek," and "——— Tate, Santa Clara." Jacob Forney to Alexander Wilson, August 10, 1859, in U. S. Cong., Senate Executive Document 32, 36th Cong., 1st Sess., 55, Serial 1031.
41. Historian's Office Journal, June 19, 1858, CR 100, 1, LDS Church Archives.
42. Hamblin to Young, Kanab, November 13, 1871; and Hamblin Statement, 1871, LDS Church Archives.
43. Bishop, ed., *Mormonism Unveiled,* 371–72; Jacob Hamblin testimony, "Second Lee Trial," LaJean Purcell Carruth transcription of the four versions of John D. Lee's second trail, pp. 246–48, 269–73, LDS Church Archives.
44. Hamblin to Young, November 13, 1871; Hamblin Statement, 1871.
45. Hamblin Statement, 1871; Hamblin to Young, November 13, 1871.
46. Hamblin Statement, 1871; Hamblin to Young, November 13, 1871.
47. Bishop, ed., *Mormonism Unveiled,* 366–67; Brooks, *Mountain Meadows Massacre,* 107–8, 121; Hamblin Statement, 1871.
48. Statement of William H. Rogers, *The Valley Tan,* February 19, 1860; Juanita Brooks, *Mountain Meadows Massacre,* 265–78.
49. Arrington, *Brigham Young,* 279.
50. Historian's Office Journal, June 24, 1858, LDS Church Archives.
51. Orson F. Whitney, *History of Utah,* 4 vols. (Salt Lake City: George Q. Cannon and Sons, 1892–1904), 1:692–706.
52. Robert N. Baskin, *Reminiscences of Early Utah* (Salt Lake City: privately printed, 1914), 135 (quotation), 117 (neglected to investigate).
53. Brooks, *Mountain Meadows Massacre,* 219.
54. Sally Denton, *American Massacre : The Tragedy at Mountain Meadows, September 11, 1857* (New York: Alfred A. Knopf, 2003), 152; for a contemporary statement of the same view see, for instance, "Argus" [Charles Wandell] "An Open Letter to Brigham Young," July 12, 1871; *The Corinne Reporter,* July 15,1871; Bagley, *Blood of the Prophets,* 380.
55. Historian's Office Journal, July 15, 16, 17, 19, 20, 21, 22, 23, and 24, 1858; and George A. Smith to Robert L. Campbell, July 29 through August 6, 1858, Collected Historical Documents [ca. 1854–1860], CR 100 397, LDS Church Archives. The latter is a letter or journal entries apparently made by Smith between July 19 and August 6, 1858.
56. Smith to Campbell, July 29 through August 6, 1858; Isaac C. Haight Journal, July 25–28, 1858, photocopy, LDS Church Archives.
57. Smith to Campbell, July 29 through August 6, 1858. Haight says they were in Harmony on August 5. Haight Journal, August 5, 1858. Lee dates their arrival in Cedar City on August 5, but Smith dates the arrival at 3:30 p.m. on August 6; Smith to Campbell, August 6, 1858; Lee, *Mormon Chronicle,* 1:179 (August 5, 1858).
58. Emily S. Hoyt, Reminiscences and Diary, 1851–1893, August 15, 1858, MS 13346, LDS Church Archives; see also Lee, *Mormon Chronicle,* 1:179 (August 6,1858).
59. Henry Lunt, "Henry Lunt Journal: Mission to England, September 9, 1854 to October 20, 1859," p. 25 (August 23 and 24, 1858), Typescript by Evelyn K and York F. Jones, Cedar City, May 1999, copy, LDS Church Archives.

60. Lee, *Mormon Chronicle*, 1:179–80 (August 5, 6, 1858). See pp. 180–81 where the entries skip from August 8 to September 15. I have been unable to find any official report of an investigation either on August 5 and 6 or 23 and 24. (See the reproduction herein.)
61. George A. Smith and James McKnight, "The Emigrant and Indian War at Mountain Meadows, Sept. 21, 22, 23, 24 and 25, 1857," Collected Historical Documents [ca 1854–1860] CR 100 397, LDS Church Archives. The account was later copied into the Journal History, where it was accessed by Juanita Brooks and others. See Brooks, *Mountain Meadows Massacre*, 242–44. Juanita Brooks described the story as "the first official report of the Mountain Meadows Massacre to Brigham Young." Brooks, *Mountain Meadows Massacre*, 165.
62. Endorsement on George A. Smith and James McKnight, "The Emigrant and Indian War At Mountain Meadows, Sept 21, 22, 23, 24, 1857," LDS Church Archives.
63. Wilford Woodruff described Lee's report to Young on September 29, 1857 as "an express," and the southern Utah leaders apparently wanted Young to consider it such. Woodruff *Journal*, 5:102 (September 29, 1857). As James Haslam demonstrated, in the days before the installation of telegraph lines, an express from southern Utah could reach Salt Lake City in just a few days. The southern Utah leaders, stewing over how to report the massacre to Young, waited some time before dispatching Lee, who arrived at Young's office eighteen days after the final massacre—hardly "an express." On October 5, 1857, Henry Lunt, then in Salt Lake, described how his father-in-law James Whittaker arrived that day from Cedar City "with a light covered wagon and a yoke of oxen and made the journey, 280 miles, in the extraordinary short space of time of nine days." "Henry Lunt Journal," 23 (October 5, 1857). Lee's arrival in a similar amount of time thus would have been considered "an express."
64. Bishop, ed., *Mormonism Unveiled*, 233–34.
65. Smith and McNight, "The Emigrant and Indian War."
66. Ibid.
67. See James McKnight's summary on the fold of "The Emigrant and Indian War" document.
68. Smith to Campbell, July 29 through August 6, 1858 ("We leave here for Parowan to-morrow morn").
69. Only James H. Martineau, stake high councilman, and Calvin C. Pendleton, Dame's first counselor, refused to join in the charges. James H. Martineau, Journal, MS 18300, August 10, 11, and 12, 1858, LDS Church Archives.
70. "Minutes of an investigation held before Geo. A. Smith and Amasa Lyman, commencing Aug. 8, 1858," Historian's Office (1842–1972) CR 100 397, Collected Historical Documents [ca. 1854–1860], LDS Church Archives.
71. "Minutes of an investigation," 1.
72. "Minutes of an investigation," 3–4; Haight Journal, August 10, 1858.
73. George A. Smith to Brigham Young, August 17, 1858, Incoming Correspondence, Brigham Young Office Files;" "Minutes of an investigation," p. 4. Haight Journal, August 12, 1858.
74. George A. Smith to Robert L. Campbell, August 15, 1858, CR 100 397, Historian's Office (1842?–1972), Collected Historical Documents [ca 1854–1860], LDS Church Archives; Historian's Office Journal, August 15, 1858, LDS Church Archives.
75. George A. Smith to Brigham Young, August 17, 1858, Letterpress copybooks 1854–1879; 1885–1886, Historian's Office (1842–1972), CR 100 38, 4:885–91, LDS Church Archives. For an interpretation of the document see Brooks, *Mountain Meadows Massacre*, 166–70. Cf. "The Emigrant and Indian War."
76. Ibid.
77. Smith and McNight, "The Emigrant and Indian War."
78. Smith to Young, August 17, 1858.
79. Ibid
80. Ibid
81. Woodruff, *Journal* 5:102.
82. Smith to Young, August 17, 1858.

83. George A. Smith to Robert L. Campbell, August 20, 1858, CR 100 397, Beaver, Historian's Office (1842?–1972), Collected Historical Documents [ca 1854–1860], LDS Archives.

84. Marion J. Shelton Diary, August 23 to September 2, 1858, excerpts, MS 14`2 fd 1, LaJean Purcell Carruth transcription of Shelton's shorthand, LDS Church Archives.

85. Lunt, "Journal," p. 25 August 23, 24, 1858. There is some discrepancy in the dating because Shelton's diary dates their travel to Cedar City on August 24 and Lunt says the investigation took place on August 23 and 24. I believe that Lunt's dating is correct since he was in Cedar City at the time. George Kirkman Bowering, Klingensmith's tithing clerk, wrote that the three apostles visited Cedar to conduct an investigation. George Kirkman Bowering, Journal, p.231 July 1842–Jan. 1875, MS 6174, LDS Church Archives.

86. Lee, *A Mormon Chronicle*, I:179 (August 5, probably August 23 or 24, 1858). Lee's Journal has entries dated through August 8, then skips to September 15, 1858. Parts of the entries purporting to be August 5 and 6 are written in a small text and may be written by another hand.

87. Shelton Diary August 23– September 2, 1858, Carruth transcription.

88. Forney used the term "Ultras" to describe the anti-Mormons.

89. On Cradlebaugh's escapades in Provo see Donald R. Moorman and Gene A. Sessions *Camp Floyd and the Mormons: The Utah War*, (Salt Lake City: University of Utah Press, 1992), 109–118. On the order prohibiting the use of the army without the governor's approval see p. 121.

90. Moorman and Sessions, *Camp Floyd*, 118; Historian's Office Journal, May 25, 1859.

91. For the information on this trial and the quotations, I have relied on Bagley, *Blood of the Prophets*, 233–34.

92. Historian's Office Journal, June 18, 1859.

93. Brigham Young, *Journal of Discourses* (March 8, 1863), (Liverpool: Daniel H. Wells, 1865), 10:110.

94. Bagley, *Blood of the Prophets*, 243.

95. Historian's Office Journal, July 5, 1859, Carruth transcription of Deseret Alphabet entry.

96. Ibid. .

97. Ibid.

98. Historian's Office Journal, May 25, June 18, and July 5, 1859, Carruth transcription of Deseret Alphabet; George A. Smith to William H. Dame, June 19, 1859, Historian's Office Letterpress copybooks 1854–1879, 1885–1886, 2:127, LDS Church Archives; Lee, *Mormon Chronicle*, 1:214 (August 5[6], 1859).

99. "Wilford Woodruff and the Mormon Reformation of 1855–57," *Dialogue: A Journal of Mormon Thought* 25 (Summer 1992): 25–39; Brigham Young and Daniel H. Wells to William H. Dame, September 14, 1857; Lee, *Mormon Chronicle*, 1:201–2 (March 14 and 18, 1859).

100. Lee, *Mormon Chronicle*, 1:201 (March 14, 1859); Shelton *Journal*, March 15, 1859, Carruth transcription.

101. Lee, *Mormon Chronicle*, 1:201–2 (March 16, 1859); Harmony Branch Minutes, March 18, 1859, Huntington Library, San Marino, CA.

102. Lee, *Mormon Chronicle*, 1:202 (March 18, 1859).

103. *Deseret News*, May 25, 1859, p. 8; also published as: "From Utah," *New York Daily Tribune*, June 24, 1859.

104. Collected Historical Documents, Historian's Office (1842–1972), CR 100 397, LDS Church Archives.

105. Manti Ward, General Minutes, 1857–59, July 13, 1859, LR 5253 11, LDS Church Archives.

106. Ibid.

107. Parowan Stake, Historical record, 1855–1860, first section, 40, July 17, 1859, LR 6778 28, LDS Church Archives.

108. Historian's Office Journal, July 15–21, 1859, LDS Church Archives.

109. Historian's Office Journal, July 15–22, 1859. *Journals of John D. Lee*, ed. Charles Kelly (Salt Lake City, University of Utah Press, 1984), 225–27. Charles Kelly, editor of this portion of the Lee Diaries also missed the message; see n. 179. Fort Harmony, Minutes, Huntington Library.

110. Kelley, *Journals of John D. Lee*, 227.
111. Lee, *Mormon Chronicle*, 1:213 (July 31, 1859). See also Historian's Office Journal, July 31, 1859. Lee, *Mormon Chronicle*, 1:213 (July 31, 1859). Philip Klingon Smith, Affidavit, April 10, 1871, in Brooks, *Mountain Meadows Massacre*, 238.
112. "Henry Lunt Journal," July 31, 1859, Cedar Stake Journal, July 31, 1859, both in Evelyn K. Jones, *Henry Lunt Biography* (Provo, UT: Privately Printed, 1996), 232–33. See also Lee, *Mormon Chronicle*, 1:213 (July 31, 1859).
113. Morris A. Shirts and Kathryn H. Shirts, *A Trial Furnace: Southern Utah's Iron Mission* (Provo, UT: Brigham Young University Press, n.d.), 397. Amasa Lyman's letter to the editor, April 14, 1859 appeared in the *Deseret News*, April 20, 1859, p. 8. Of Cedar City, however, he noted, "Many of the people of this city are removing to other localities, in consequence of the suspension of the Iron works and the want of water to sustain them by farming."
114. Arrington, *Brigham Young*, 279,
115. Haight Journal, July 31, 1859.
116. Philip Klingensmith to George A. Smith, August 1, 1859, George A. Smith Papers, LDS Church Archives.
117. Lee, *Mormon Chronicle*, 1:214 (August 5 [6], 1859).
118. Lee, *Mormon Chronicle*, 1:219 (September 11, 1859).
119. George A. Smith to Isaac C. Haight, November 6, 1859, Historian's Office letterbook, 1:845–46, LDS Church Archives. I was not able to locate Haight's letter; the information on the retainer, which Smith was unable to find, comes from Smith's letter.
120. Alexander Wilson to Jeremiah Black, November 15, 1859, Senate Executive Document 32, 36th Cong., 1st Sess., 41, Serial 1031.
121. D. R. Eckels to Lewis Cass, September 27, 1859, Office Files, 1832–1878 (bulk 1844–1877, Brigham Young Papers, box 28, fd. 41, LDS Church Archives.
122. Ibid
123. Eckels to Cass, September 27, 1859. "Federal Courts and Judges," *Deseret News*, September 7, 1859, July 8, 1863.
124. *Deseret News*, September 7, 1859; Eckels to Cass, September 27, 1859. John Cradlebaugh and Charles E. Sinclair to James Buchanan, July 16, 1859, in Senate, *Message of the President*, S. Doc. 32, pp. 19–20.
125. "First Judicial District Court," *Deseret News*, September 7, 1859; Eckels to Cass, September 27, 1859.
126. Stephen DeWolfe to Alexander Wilson, August 28, 1859, quoted in Wilson to Jeremiah Black, November 15, 1859 in U. S. Cong., Senate Executive Document 32, 36th Cong., 1st Sess., 32, Serial 1031.
127. Wilson to Black, November 15, 1859, U.S. Cong., Senate Executive Document 32, 36th Cong., 1st Sess., 42, Serial 1031.
128. Jacob Forney to A. B. Greenwood, September 22, 1859, in Senate Executive Document 42, 36th Cong., 1st Sess., 86, Serial 1033. Those "most guilty," he believed, were Haight, Klingensmith, Lee, Higbee, "Bishop [William R.] Davis," David Tullis, and Ira Hatch. "These were the cause of the massacre," he charged, "aided by others."
129. Brigham Young, President's Office Journal, Dec. 1857–Jan. 1860, and September 2, 1859, CR 1234 2, LDS Church Archives.
130. "The Court at Nephi," *Deseret News*, September 14, 1859.
131. Eckels to Cass, September 27, 1859.
132. Lewis Cass to Alfred Cumming, December 2, 1859, 1859 Correspondence, Alfred Cumming Papers, Duke University Library, Durham, NC. Alfred Cumming to Lewis Cass, February 2, 1860, in Letterpress Book, Cumming Papers, (on reverse side of 1:476–92; also in 2:127–41).
133. Brigham Young to Hiram McKee, May 3, 1860, Brigham Young Letter Book, 5:493, Brigham Young Office Files, LDS Church Archives.
134. Woodruff, *Journal*, 5:577 (May 25, 1861).
135. Lee, *Mormon Chronicle*, 1:314 (May 31 [30], 1861).

136. Brigham Young address, March 8, 1863, in *Journal of Discourses*, 26 vols. (Liverpool: F. D. Richards, 1855–1886), 10:110.

137. David John Journals, May 6, 1862 [1863], vol. 3:60, MS 21, L. Tom Perry Special Collections, Harold B. Lee Library, Brigham Young University, Provo, Utah. John's account of the trip appears in his journal for 1889, where he copied entries from an old journal on a trip that he experienced with Church leaders (3:52). He misdated the information in recopying it. In the journal, he dates the events in 1862, but they actually occurred in 1863. Confusion in the dating is resolved by comparison with contemporaneous accounts of the trip in the following sources: Alonzo H. Raleigh Diary, 1861–1885, photocopy, MS Sc 360, L. Tom Perry Special Collections, Harold B. Lee Library, Brigham Young University, Provo, Utah; and L. O. Littlefield, letter to the editor, April 7, 1863, *Deseret News*, May 20, 1863. See also Lorenzo Brown, Journal, April 29, May 7, 8, 11, 12, 1863, MS 4957, LDS Church Archives.

138. David John, Journal, May 6, [1863], vol. 3:60, Special Collections, BYU Library. According to Mel Bashore, "A descendant of David John transcribed the journal . . . He incorrectly cited it as 1862 but BY [Brigham Young] was in SLC in 1862" (Mel Bashore to Brian Reeves, January 23, 2006). Lyman O. Littlefield reported BY's entourage as being in Washington in the *Deseret News* on that date.

139. R. N. Baskin, closing argument, August 5, 1875, "First Trial of John D. Lee," LaJean Purcell Carruth transcription of the four versions of John D. Lee's first trial, p. 345, LDS Church Archives.

140. Erastus Snow, affidavit, February 21, 1882, in Charles W. Penrose, *The Mountain Meadows Massacre. Who Were Guilty of the Crime?* (Salt Lake City: Juvenile Instructor Office, 1884), 67.

141. "Thirty-Third Annual Conference," *Deseret News*, April 22, 1863, p. 1.

142. "Conversation between Col Potter, Capt Grimes and Prest Young on establishment of liquor saloons," May 8, 1866, Brigham Young, Office Files, 1832–1878 (bulk 1844–1877), CR 1234 1, box 49, fd. 28, LDS Church Archives.

143. Brigham Young, address, December 23, 1866, in "Remarks," *Deseret News*, January 9, 1867, p. 3.

144. Brigham Young to George A. Hicks, February 16, 1869, Brigham Young Letters Sent, 11: 362–363, Brigham Young Office Files, LDS Church Archives.

145. Lee, *Mormon Chronicle*, 2:18–19 (June 9, 1866; 2:20–21), 2: 71–73 (June 22, 1866; 2: 71–73), 2: 88–89, 96 (May 14, 17, 19, 23 [these entries are dated one day too soon; June 10 [11], 1867); 2: 88–89, 96, (November 4, 16 [14], 1867); 2: 96, (January 26 [25] 1868) [the entry dates are off as indicated] . In a public meeting in September, Snow "strongly vindicated the rights of the Red men." Lee, *Mormon Chronicle*, 2:28 (September 14, 1866).

146. George A. Smith to Mr. St. Clair, November 25, 1869, Historian's Office (1842–1972) Letterpress copybooks, 1854–1879; 1885–1886, vol. 2: 941–49, LDS Church Archives.

147. Smith to St. Clair, November 25, 1869.

148. *Mormon Chronicle*, 2:134 (March 9, 1870); 2: 138, (September 7 [9], 1870).

149. Erastus Snow, affidavit, February 21, 1882, in Charles W. Penrose, *The Mountain Meadows Massacre: Who Were Guilty of the Crime?* (Salt Lake City: Juvenile Instructor Office, 1884), 67–68.

150. Snow, affidavit, February 21, 1882, in Penrose, *Mountain Meadows Massacre*, 68. On the conversation with Lorenzo Roundy and Nephi Johnson see John R. Young to Susa Y. Gates, June 1, 1927, John Ray Young, Scrapbook, 1928–1930, pp.109–10, MS 1180 2, LDS Church Archives. See also John R. Young to W. S. Erekson, February 1928, Collected material concerning the Mountain Meadows Massacre, MS 2674, LDS Church Archives. John R. Young, writing many decades after the fact in 1927 and 1928, placed this event in 1865, a year in which Young did in fact visit southern Utah. The totality of the evidence, however, including Nephi Johnson's testimony, suggests that the event occurred in 1870. In an interview with a newspaper reporter in 1877, Young said concerning the massacre, "I never knew the real facts of this affair untill within the last few years." "Brigham Young: Remarkable Interview with the Salt Lake Prophet," *New York Herald*, May 6, 1877.

151. "President Young and Party," *Deseret Evening News*, September 19, 1870.
152. Young to Gates, June 1, 1927, Young Scrapbook, p. 110; Young to Erekson, February 1928.
153. Nephi Johnson affidavit, July 22, 1908, First Presidency, Cumulative Correspondence, 1900–1949, box 7, fd. 10, Mountain Meadows, CR 1 33, LDS Church Archives.
154. Nephi Johnson, affidavit, July 22, 1908; conversation with Anthony W. Ivins, September 12, 1917, typescript, Anthony W. Ivins collection, box 14, fd. 11, Utah State Historical Society; John W. Bradshaw testimony, first Lee trial, Boreman version, book 5:2, Carruth-Johnson transcription. On those who went because they believed they were going to save the emigrants see testimony of Samuel McMurdy in Bishop, ed., *Mormonism Unveiled*, 340. See also Johnson testimony in Bishop, ed., *Mormonism Unveiled*, 346–47.
155. Brigham Young to Horace S. Eldredge, October 4, 1870, Brigham Young Letter Book, 12:396, Brigham Young Office Files, LDS Church Archives.
156. Snow, affidavit, February 21, 1882, in Penrose, *Mountain Meadows Massacre*, 68. Wilford Woodruff, Joseph F. Smith, and Franklin D. Richards reported the council meeting and the excommunications of Lee and Haight in their journals. Woodruff *Journal*, 6:574 (October 8, 1870). Joseph F. Smith, Journal, October 8, 1870, MS 1325, box 2, fd. 8, LDS Church Archives. Franklin D. Richards Journal, October 9, 1870, MS 1215 box 2, fd. 3, v. 18, LDS Church Archives. The minutes of the meeting in which Lee was excommunicated, along with other early minutes of the Quorum of the Twelve, burned in the tragic Council House fire of June 21, 1883. William W. Taylor to the Presidency and Members of the High Council of the Salt Lake Stake of Zion, July 6, 1883, in Salt Lake Stake, Report regarding destruction of stake records, LDS Church Archives.
157. Lee, *Mormon Chronicle,* 2:143–44 (November 17, 1870); Juanita Brooks, *John Doyle Lee: Zealot, Pioneer Builder, Scapegoat* (Salt Lake City: Howe Brothers, 1874), 293–95. *Mormon Chronicle,* 2:145, 150, 151, 155, 156, 157–58 (November 19, December 19 [21],1870, January 6, 7, and March 6, 20, 1871).
158. Lee, *Mormon Chronicle,* 2:146 (November 22, 1870).
159. Lee, *Mormon Chronicle,* 2:146–47 (November 22, 1870).
160. Brooks, *Mountain Meadows Massacre*, 184.
161. Bagley, *Blood of the Prophets*, 271–75.
162. Lee, *Mormon Chronicle,* 2:151–52 (December 29 [22], 1870).
163. Lee, *Mormon Chronicle,* 2:152 (December 1870). The dates in Lee's journal are off. Lee dates this the twenty-ninth, but he says that it is Thursday, which would be the twenty-second; also the next entry is dated the Sunday the twenty-third. Brooks corrects it to the twenty-fifth.
164. Ibid.
165. Lee, *Mormon Chronicle,* 2:153–54 (December 28, 1870). Snow reports of this incident, "During the following Winter, while Presidents Brigham Young and George A. Smith were at my home in St. George, Lee made application to me to intercede for him to obtain an interview with them; but when I spoke to them about it they both positively declined to see him or receive any communication from him." Snow, affidavit, February 21, 1882, in Penrose, *Mountain Meadows Massacre*, 68.
166. Lee, *Mormon Chronicle,* 2:153 (December 27, 1870).
167. Ibid
168. Lee, *Mormon Chronicle,* 2:154 (January 3 [2], 1871). On Willis as Roundy's counselor, see Kanarra Ward, Cedar West Stake, Manuscript history and historical reports, LDS Church Archives.
169. John Bringhurst, statement, July 27, 1928, Collected material concerning the Mountain Meadows Massacre, MS 2674, fd. 27, LDS Church Archives.
170. Christopher J. Arthur, "Records of Christopher J. Arthur, 1860–1900, typescript, part 4, LDS Church Archives. "Isaac C. Haight was rebaptized some years afterwards and afterwards officiated in the Manti Temple and figured prominently in Church affairs in New Mexico, Colorado, Mexico, etc." John D. Lee Sketch, Biographical sketches, MS 17956, Andrew Jenson Collection, LDS Church Archives.

171. Christopher J. Arthur, "Records," 4:34; The date of March 3, 1874, is based on the information in Arthur on the death of Caroline Haight Arthur. On March 8, 1874 Toquerville was organized in the United Order . . . Subsequently Isaac C. Haight was chosen as an appraiser. Toquerville Ward, Zion Park State, Manuscript history and historical reports, 1874, Church Archives.

172. Roberts, *Comprehensive History*, 4:178n30.

173. Brigham Young to William W. Belknap, May 21, 1872, Letters Received by the Office of the Adjutant General (Main Series) 1871–80, RG 94, Microfilm 619A, Roll 32, 1871.

174. Ibid.

175. Lee, *Mormon Chronicle*, 2:336 (April 5, 1874).

176. Eli Perkins interview with Brigham Young, May 12, 1877, published as "Brigham Young: A Long Talk with the Prophet," *New York Times*, May 20, 1877. See the same story in William Booth Ashworth, Autobiography, p. 106, Typescript: n.p., n.d., MS 801, LDS Church Archives.

177. According to Robert N. Baskin, in the first trial, the U. S. Attorney, William Carey; his assistant, D. P. Whedon; and Baskin declined to prosecute Dame because they did not have sufficient evidence against him. Richard E. Turley, Jr., "John D. Lee's First Trial," p. 32, MS in author's possession, n.d. In the second trial, Sumner Howard said that he had insufficient evidence to try Dame. Presumably, the same situation applied to Willden and Adair. Bagley, *Blood of the Prophets*, 301. On Lee's comment see Kelly, *Journals of John D. Lee*, 203.

178. See copies of the affidavits in Bishop, ed. *Mormonism Unveiled*, 309–14.

179. See Richard E. Turley, Jr., "John D. Lee's First Trial," *passim*.

180. "Federal Courts and Judges," *Deseret News,* July 8, 1863. For an example see John Jaques to George Q. Cannon, June 30, 1859, Historian's Office Letter Book 1:789–90. Alfred Cumming also complained that the federal judges and U. S. Marshal refused to recognize the authority of the probate judges. Cumming to Cass, February 2, 1860.